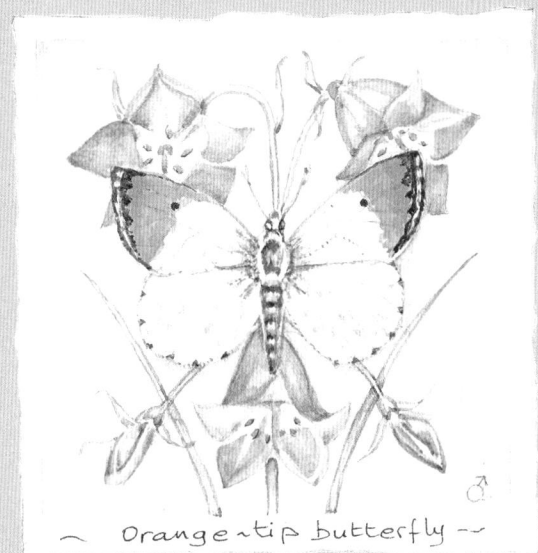

~ Orange-tip butterfly ~

~ Orange-tip butterfly ~

The
Majical World
of
John Clare

John Clare

The Majical World of John Clare.

CLARE'S SEASONS

A selection of John Clare's writings ∼
from his unique observation of RURAL LIFE
as depicted in his masterpiece

THE SHEPHERD'S CALENDAR
plus extracts from his
JOURNAL 1824 - 25
to which is added
POEMS
SONNETS
ESSAYS
& LETTERS

carefully chosen to supplement the rhythm
of the passing year and showing his deep
love and understanding for all living things
in the NATURAL WORLD.

by
Marianna Kneller
2014

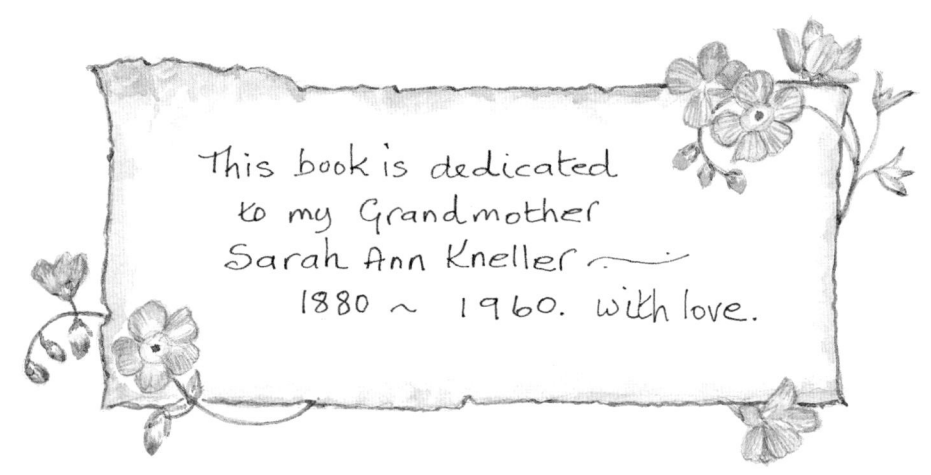

This book is dedicated
to my Grandmother
Sarah Ann Kneller ~
1880 ~ 1960. with love.

PUBLICATION DETAILS

First published 2014
Hand-written script and illustrations copyright © 2014 Marianna Kneller.
Foreword © Ronald Blythe
Portrait of John Clare, W. Hilton © National Portrait Gallery NPG1469

Photo typesetting, colour separation, printed by Healeys Print Group,
Ipswich, Suffolk. IP1 5AP

British Library Cataloguing in Publication Data

ISBN

978 0 9563162 88

ACKNOWLEDGEMENTS.

I would like to say thank you to the many people who gave so generously their time, encouragement and support over the years it has taken to create this book.

Marcia Gattrell, Nurse Hyde, and Elsie Wilcox for their early influences.

Daphne Gallagher, Rosemary Seys, Margaret Stevens, Margaret Webb and Dr. Margaret Whitby, for their assistance at crucial times.

Yinnen & Ruth Baron Ezra, Sir Andrew Motion, Dr. Janet Owen, & Evelyn Thurlby, whose professional directions and suggestions were so freely given.

Dr. Ronnie Blythe & Dr. Simon Kövesi, of The John Clare Society.

Robert Wilson of the Northamptonshire Flora Group, whose invaluable help with "Druce's Flora of Northamptonshire," added another dimension to the content of this book.

To my many friends at Exbury and beyond, who joined in the adventure of 'finding Clare'. Jenny Caplin, Jo Friendship, Doug and Margot Harris, Sylvia Lovell, Tom Kellam, Linda Runnacles and the 4SA group.

Gill Robinson for all her advice.

Sylvia Goulding for her specialist help.

SPECIAL THANKS TO

the Rothschild family, especially Mr. Eddy, Nicholas and Lionel de Rothschild, whose Gardens at Exbury provided the flowers, inspiration and so much more.

Christine Thwaites, for her constant support,

and to Reggie A. Roberts
for always being 'there'.

The little blue forget-me-not
Comes too on friendship's gentle plea,
Spring's messenger in every spot,
Smiling on all
'Remember Me'!
'On a May Morning.' John Clare.

Majic

John Clare was mainly self taught, his only education bought by the precious pennies paid to a Dames School in his home village of Helpston, and then at Mr. Seaton's makeshift schoolroom in the Vestry of St. Benedict's at Glinton in the county of Northamptonshire.

His very personal spelling and punctuation has been subject of much debate. In the main I have followed by instinct, his original spelling and dialect, with a few corrections made by his editor and publisher John Taylor where I have thought it appropriate.

Of particular note for this book is his spelling of the word 'magic'. As Simon Kövesi writes in his edition of *John Clare, Flower Poems*, "In his manuscripts the word 'magic' is spelled 'majic'; perhaps Clare intended just such a distancing effect of antiquity and mystery that is conveyed immediately we see 'majic' but not when we read 'magic'".

FINDING CLARE

The past it is a majic word
Too beautiful to last
It looks back like a lovely face –
Who can forget the past?
There's music in its childhood
That's known in every tongue,
Like the music of the wildwood
All chorus to the song …
John Clare, *Childhood, v1*

It lay in my hand, the most beautiful thing I had ever seen, smooth, warm, so very light, fragile and of a most exquisite colour, a turquoise-blue, spattered with black freckles. It nestled very comfortably in my small palm and I felt so overwhelmed with the wonder of it.

"We must put it back carefully before the mother returns, otherwise she'll be very upset", said Miss Hyde, our young nurse. This was the moment nature first touched my soul. I was four years old. We were out on our afternoon walk, a small straggly crocodile file of toddlers who had been evacuated to the safety of the countryside. I loved those walks. When you're young, everything on the ground is so close to you, tiny things are easily observed, so much to see.

It was spring, the cold of the winter had passed, the sunbeams twinkled and dazzled, lighting everything into a fairyland of moving light; and now this extra wonderment, all so very new.

"It's a thrush's egg, there's a baby bird growing in it."

A brood of nature's minstrels chirp and fly,
Glad as the sunshine and laughing sky

wrote John Clare in his poem 'The Thrushes Nest'.

These words rekindled that moment in my childhood. I remember wanting to keep the egg and cry. It was all too beautiful.

In the summertime, after the midday meal was finished and the children's afternoon nap over, the funny little canvas beds were folded and stacked away, the sprinkler system would be set out on the lawns and turned on, sending the water swishing and hissing up and around. After the initial shock of cold water it became one of the most enjoyable of times, full of shrieks and squeals of laughter; but more entrancing were the fine arcs of colour formed by sunbeams reflecting off the misty droplets of water. We were surrounded with the majical colours of rainbows. As we danced the grass below tickled our toes.

The days grew shorter and colder – no more sleeping outside on the lawns. Instead, we were bundled into too-large coats and knitted hats and scarves. Shuffling through the leaves on the path, I stopped to look at a furry animal sitting on a tree stump. It was nibbling at something, twisting and turning it to get a better bite.

"That's a squirrel, it will hide some nuts in a hole, storing them to eat through the winter." It flicked and twitched its tail and stared right into my eyes. Just as I turned to catch up with the crocodile file, there was a noise so strange and different and so loud, that as it came closer I held my breath, fearful and transfixed as huge horses huffing loudly, dogs barking, men shouting, horn sounding, all thundered by in a rush. It was the colours that amazed me.

> And hunters, from the thicket's avenue,
> In scarlet jackets, startling on the view
> *Shepherd's Calendar – October*

A swirl of reds and whites, blacks and browns and brightly coloured leaves flying everywhere – along with the squirrel that dashed up a tree.

> The squirrel sputters up the powdered oak
> With tail cocked over his head and ears erect.
> *Shepherd's Calendar – October*

I was off after them, running as fast as I could as they disappeared through the trees. Arms closed around me, my legs still kicking trying to run and catch up with the colours. Then they were gone, just the very quiet of the woods remained. All these years later, I can close my eyes and see that moving swirl of colours – glorious.

It was freezing cold. I looked over the vast white lawns stretching towards the trees, made black in contrast to the snow, that lay pristine, undulating and sparkling in small sequins, glistening in the sunlight.

> A landscape to the aching sight,
> A vast expanse of dazzling light
> *The Winter's Spring*

The war ended. I went to live with my grandmother. As with other members of my family, she too had lost her home with the bombing, but had now been rehoused.

"Are you my Fairy Godmother?" I had asked when we first met. "No, I am your Grandmother. You can call me Granny, but not Nanny, that's a billy goat's mother." Later she took me into her garden and showed me a large, rain-sprinkled, blue flower, back-lit by the sun. From the middle of a cobweb she gently removed and held a spider. Stroking its end part (the spinneret) with the tip of her finger, she carefully drew out a length of pure gossamer silk. Then, with the spider suspended, she gently replaced it onto its web … Majic!

"And we live in Iris Road, which is also the name of this flower. Can you remember that?" Could I?! My new home was in a flower … Majic!

All the neighbouring roads were named after flowers. My friends lived in Aster, Begonia, Lilac, Pansy and Primrose Roads, Bluebell Road (where my parents had lost their home), Carnation, Laburnum, Lobelia, Lupin and Poppy were on the far side of the recreation grounds which we never crossed or played in. It was far too tame, boring. I went to school in Honeysuckle Road and on Sundays to the church in Tulip Road. But the road I loved best was Violet Road. It led to the 'copse' as we called it.

The copse had been a small estate and farm, requisitioned by the American Army preparing for the Normandy Landings but then abandoned to nature. Trenches criss-crossed acres of ground, which had become overgrown with brambles that formed tunnels and became our dens. An old white-starred American jeep, deep brown, matched the bog it rested in. With the brilliant contrast of the sky-blue forget-me-nots 'eyed with a pin's head yellow spot i' the middle of its tender blue', nestling in and fringing the vacant wheel hubs, this became our pirate ship. Streams were dammed and frogspawn and tadpoles collected in jam jars. A path, its surface worn to a fine silvery-smooth sand where lizards ran and flicked their way to safety, leaving feathery imprints behind them, led to the higher grounds, weaving through the bluebell woods and pine and chestnut trees.

Then there were the oak trees. I lived in the tops of them. Sometimes I sat up there in the sky, away in my own day-dreamy world, with the quiet rustling leaves as company and looked out over the town towards the docks, listening to the deep throaty horns of the 'Queens' as they sailed along the Southampton Water.

Just three miles away, in the same direction, a middle-aged man was unlocking his shop. It had been boarded up at the beginning of the war. On entering he could hardly move for the books that he had hastily bought from another bookseller, who had been desperate to leave the town before the start of hostilities. The shop now, with all the others in the terrace, leaned to the east, the result of a bomb which had destroyed the buildings opposite. He turned the key and entered …

There were moments in my childhood where I walked with John Clare. I remember thinking, "Look at that, isn't it marvellous?" – who was asking the question, myself or something, someone prompting me, making me pause, observe and wonder? It was majical to lay flattened on the hay-ready grass, turning my head, so that my eye could be closer to the ground. I could look at the complex structures of roots and growth of many plants and the life teeming within them. Grasshoppers and beetles were fascinating to watch, strange and comical as they shifted, shimmered and jumped, scurrying along with their business of living, completely unaware of my fixed stare as I intruded on their lives.

A most extraordinary, beautiful memory that I have been blessed with is one of a hot day in a week of blistering sunshine which had warmed the earth in the meadow that edged along a stretch of bank in the lower reaches of the River Test. It was a favourite spot for the children to swim and play in their summer holidays. On this day, the tide was at its zenith, overflowing the banks onto the meadowland for hundreds of yards, lapping around the base of the pylons and edging closer to the gardens which were the boundary of the village. Sitting quietly by myself in the flooded grass, with the earth-warmed water lapping around my waist, I could see the meadow grasses and flowers protruding above their mirrored images; whole swathes of buttercups reflecting gold and clover floating bottle-like, bobbing in the wake caused by the mallard ducks who were busily gobbling up everything. Here and there were moon daisies with vetches delicately clinging to them. Everything above the waterline became a safe haven for the insects, islands of colour with butterflies and bees continuing in their search for pollen and nectar, with the non-flyers holding on perilously to the rafts of grassy flotsam caught up momentarily in the gentle flow of the rising water. They appeared numerous; I looked at this wonder of teeming life around me and the scent of the clover, sweet in the summer air, was intoxicating.

> ... The past – there lies in that one word
> Joys more than wealth can crown
> Nor could a million call them back
> Though muses wrote them down;
> The sweetest joys imagined yet,
> The beauties that surpassed
> All life or fancy ever met
> Are there among the past.
> John Clare, *Childhood*, v55

Now to leave the childhood dreams and times behind. Or, do we, ... ever?

Steve, my partner, and I bought the eastward-leaning shop* with its thousands of books in 1975. We moved in with two cats, a dog and our own large collection of books.

There were six rooms, a basement that extended under the pavement, plus two flights of stairs, all shelved and bulging with books; also, a courtyard and an outside Victorian toilet and two very large sheds stacked high with the overflow of more stock.

We pushed and piled boxes of books against the book-lined walls of an upstairs room to make space for the bed, a small table and TV set; then lit the fire and choked on the smoke that billowed out.

It was November, very cold and damp, a heavy fog pressed against the windows, all was gloom, lit only with a single, shadeless, low-watt bulb.

It felt very strange and other-worldly.

I lay in bed shivering, wondering what on earth we had done, but as I peered at the books on the shelves, the titles and authors' names wrapped around me, all with something to say; it was friendly and comforting. A new beginning?

Four years later, on a rainy November day, I began painting my first flower at the table in the shop. It was a vibrant magenta-coloured azalea defying the winter's gloom. The next week I bought another, a deep rosy-red, which proved to be quite a challenge.

A regular customer, Mr McKinlay from Edinburgh, who loved books on fly-fishing, curiously looked over my shoulder and asked if I liked azaleas? "Yes", I replied. "You want to visit Exbury, they grow beautiful azaleas there," he suggested.

So, still in November, and thinking Exbury was a supplier to the florist trade, I telephoned their office and tentatively asked if they had any azaleas? There was a pause before the reply – a little chuckle, then, "A few, and a few rhododendrons as well?" "No, sorry", I said, "I'm not interested in rhododendrons."

For the next 25 years, I painted rhododendrons.

Later, in the same month, with a pink-and-white-frilled azalea in front of me, another customer looked over my shoulder at the paintings and suggested they should be exhibited at the Royal Horticultural Society in London. "Give them my name as a reference", she said. This was Pandora Sellers, who became Kew Gardens' top artist and went on to paint their magnificent collection of tropical orchids. I knew as I looked into her extraordinary turquoise-aquamarine eyes, that I would respond to her suggestion.

The following February, at the RHS exhibition in London, my azalea paintings received the Grenfell Medal for Botanical Art. Here I met a group of dedicated artists with a range of special botanical interests, from the tiniest of lichens, fungi and wild flowers to exotic horticultural wonders; some were awarded the precious RHS Gold Medal for their work. Their freely given help and encouragement opened my eyes to a very different world.

I never met Mr McKinlay or Pandora again.

Looking back, it was strange how it all came together. From that telephone call to Exbury came an invitation to visit them in the New Year.

It wasn't just a plant nursery after all, but a 200-acre woodland garden that lies between the New Forest in Hampshire and the shoreline of the Solent, home to the Rothschild's collection of rhododendrons, azaleas and camellias.

I took a portfolio of azalea paintings with me, and had tea and fruit cake with the Gardens' Manager, Douglas Harris. He was to be my mentor, and somehow in spring 1980, I moved into a small purpose-built studio in their newly opened Plant Centre. Exbury Gardens were having to adapt to the increasing number of garden visitors and plant buyers. Times were changing.

The first morning, May Day, I turned the key in The Studio's door, entered and breathed in the scent of warm pinewood and paint, then set the drawing board, water jar, paper, brushes and two old boxes of paints on the table, to prepare for the day and the first visitors. It was the beginning of a routine I was to follow for the next 24 years, as, along with the cuckoo, I arrived every spring to open The Studio in the Gardens at Exbury.

The door opened and a slightly hesitant but broadly smiling man came in and introduced himself as Dougie Betteridge, the Head Gardener, who was to become another great friend. "I've come to show you around."

He whisked me into the Gardens in his battered and rusty old van with a very crashing gearbox, for a quick tour. I couldn't believe my eyes.

My initial tour with Doug Harris, in the January a few weeks before, had left me with a lasting impression of everything being a dark green blur. The cedar, pine, fir trees and tall rhododendron bushes, became a backdrop to the theatre stage now set before me. Colour, colour and more colour: it was spectacular. I held onto my seat as we whizzed, twisted and bumped around some very narrow gravelly paths, a kaleidoscope of moving patterns blurred together. I was overwhelmed.

We stopped, so I could choose a flower or two, but where to start? Like a child loose in a sweet shop, I wanted to have them all. Completely overawed, I returned to the studio with my first selection, a rhododendron and – a primrose.

One morning, two years on, Dougie came in with his usual tempting choice of his 'flower of the day', his enthusiasm always infectious. "This is my favourite of all time, it's called the *yakushimanum*", and he laid it carefully down on the table in front of me. Its beauty made my heart miss a beat, such quiet perfection, how can Nature create such as this? I was in love. "It's a rhododendron species from Japan", Dougie said, disappearing out of the door.

It was my introduction to the wild rhododendron species, Mother Nature's own, that had been found and collected by plant hunters in expeditions from all over the world.

I started painting them from the specimens growing at Exbury and then from other specialist gardens from all over the UK, helped by enthusiasts from around the world. Eventually, in 1996, *The Book of Rhododendrons* was published.

But I was torn: how, in my wanderings in the Gardens, could I ignore the gentle, quiet, unassuming wildflowers, when such care had to be taken not to crush them underfoot? They formed carpets of colour everywhere. Springtime is their time; in their home environment, of course, they had to be noticed.

When collecting *Rhododendron griersonianum*, a most spectacular geranium-scarlet rhododendron, originally from the pine forests of Yunnan, China, I found it in an embrace with our wild honeysuckle, their combined scents creating a heady intoxicating perfume and sending the bumblebees frantic in ecstatic activity. And the rich honey-smelling yellow *Rhododendron luteum*, from the Caucasus Mountains, rested flowering branches onto beds of bluebells, making one's eyes 'jazz'.

Later, in the summertime, as I collected the new leaf growth of the rhododendrons, the Gardens' meadowlands along the banks of the Beaulieu River, flowered profusely with ragged robin, fleabane, yellow rattle, clover, orchids, vetches and many others, all irresistible to the meadow butterflies which danced their days away. Here the skylarks nested, flew and sang, till they disappeared, as small as a pin's head, into the open sky, and the curlew's beautiful haunting call accompanied the walkers following the river's path. Once, two small boys pulled their father into The Studio, to tell me excitedly they had seen an osprey, on its journey northwards, touch down on the river to catch a fish.

And in autumn, when the rhododendron seed capsules plumped and ripened in their candelabra-like appearance, they had to be painted as well; but so did the berries and chestnuts, fallen leaves and so on, I couldn't not paint them all, could I?

Then winter, the truly magical, mystical waiting time of the year. Everywhere so quiet that you could hear the ice fracturing on the twigs, as the weak sunlight teased a response, and if it warmed just a fraction more, the water droplets took on all the colours of the spectrum and everywhere turned into a living jewel box. What a wonder of countryside we have.

I felt dissatisfied. It was another November, four years later … raining again. I needed a project for the winter – something for The Studio's visitors, a small book with wild flower paintings, with poetry perhaps?

On the table in front of me, two large cardboard boxes of books wrestled up the stairs from the basement, with their dusty lids tied with string. Anthologies – they may be useful?

The slanting heavy rain hit the windows with force, and not content with that, it found its way into little channels through the badly-in-need-of-repair-roof and fell pinging and plopping into the various containers placed around the floor. It was so annoying, there's nothing more depressing than the sound of rainwater falling … indoors.

I selected a book, glanced at the index, riffled through the pages, looking for even the slightest inspiration, nothing; the next pile, nothing. What was I searching for? Something, anything! The rejected pile on the table grew higher, I felt even more dissatisfied, very November-ish, bored.

Then, a Day Book, personal daily jottings of this and that. Intrigued I opened its brown-edged pages, some pressed flowers, hand-written notes and poems. I carefully turned the pages not wanting to dislodge the fragile dried flowers – a flattened transparent snowdrop, forget-me-nots, still with a hint of blue, a four-leaf clover – all with their shadowy browned image pressed into the paper; poems, more poems, another poem. I started to read.

Come hither, my dear one, my choice one, and rare one,

What a compelling first line. The words beckoned me on.

And let us be walking the meadows so fair,

An image of waving grass and flowers, blue sky, an English meadow, I felt a little sad.

Where on pilewort and daisies the eye fondly gazes,
And the wind plays so sweet on thy bonny brown hair,

My grandmother was of Scottish descent, and she would sing to me, "I love a lassie, a bonny, bonny lassie", making me feel very special to her. I read on transfixed.

Come with thy maiden eye, lay silks and satins by;
Come in thy russet or grey cotton gown;
Come to the meads, dear, where flags, sedge, and reeds appear,
Rustling to soft winds and bowing low down.

November disappeared into another time, the falling rain fell quietly. I held my breath, feeling even sadder. I felt somewhere else.

Come with thy parted hair, bright eyes, and forehead bare;
Come to the whitethorn that grows in the lane;
To banks of primroses, where sweetness reposes,
Come, love, and let us be happy again …

I could smell primroses.

Here was someone who, through his words, said what we can all feel, the need to go back to a time in one's life, to feel that perfect connection with the world, with a loved one, with life, and that the happiness will last forever. A wish – so sad.

I looked at the name under the poem … John Clare.

John who?

I am hoping this book will introduce the poet John Clare and his remarkable work to people who have never heard of him.

In the many years since Clare came into my life, whenever I mentioned his name to visitors at The Studio at Exbury, they looked at me blankly, with no recollection of ever having heard his name or knowing of his existence. Yet when they looked at my paintings along with his beautiful words, they immediately took to him and wanted to know more about him and his extraordinary life.

I fell into that category. Until that bleak rainy November day in 1986, I had been totally unaware of Clare, yet having read the poem, accidentally found, I knew that he was a special person. An English 'National Treasure' to be taken into one's heart.

That morning, I immediately needed to find out more about him. My brother worked at the Southampton University Library, but he could only find three books and one had last been taken out over a year before. But they were enough, and for the next three months I avidly wrote down ideas, and selected poems and the prose that inspired me. I also sketched ideas for illustrations and drafted layout designs. This had to be laid to one side as another book had to be completed first, though whenever an opportunity presented itself in the form of a beautiful wild flower, I couldn't resist the temptation to safely record it in my notebook for future reference.

John Clare can be all things to all people, but for me, I fell in love with his care for all living things. He came into my life unexpectedly, with all the gentle promise of an early spring day with a hint of the summer to come. He is so very much of our countryside.

It is very easy to find John Clare. If there's a wild flower blooming, a bird singing, a beautiful dawn, or a crescent moon hanging high in the night's sky – then he's there – everywhere.

The original manuscript I worked on all those years ago is very tatty now, well thumbed and scribbled over. Yet when I open it the same overwhelming excitement and enthusiasm is still there. This is what I hope you will experience as you turn the pages in this book.

The poem opposite that inspired me all those years ago is so simple, almost song-like.

It's called 'The Invitation'. I accepted. I hope you, too, will join with me in this book.

Marianna

---

* The elderly gentleman, who had wished us "Good Luck" when handing over the keys to the eastward-leaning bookshop, was Mr Charles Fenwick Skrimshire. The man who was responsible for John Clare's wellbeing and care for many years was Dr Fenwick Skrimshire. "Skrimshire was a man of varied accomplishments, not all of them medical. He shared Clare's interest in natural history and in the study of birds' eggs in particular" (Jonathan Bate, *John Clare: A Biography*).

Thomas Hoods affectionate account of Clare as
"Our Green Man, with his bright, grass~coloured coat and
yellow waist~coat. So slight he was in frame, so del~
icate in complexion and sensibilities, that I considered
him insufficiently rough to seem like a true rustic
~ he was more cowslip than cowherd'.

Thomas Hood's *Literary Reminiscenses*
1822

Introducing John Clare

One might daringly claim that no other major English writer is as much a part of us as John Clare. A prolific poet-naturalist, his work is in some ways our biography as well as his. He shared the same publisher as John Keats and he died a few months before W.B. Yeats was born. These years were an amazing time for poetry. And yet he remains 'alone', and would remain so until the late twentieth century when he would influence Seamus Heaney, Ted Hughes and naturalists like Richard Mabey. By which time the traditional thousand years old countryside which he knew had passed away and he had become its most inspired remembrancer.

John Clare was born in Helpston in 1793, an ancient haphazard village full of wild places then, but which would soon suffer 'progress' in the form of the industrial revolution, when the 'poor' lost their ancient rights and ended up in the workhouse. He was taught to read and write in a church vestry, and his first poet was James Thomson whose 'Seasons' was an eighteenth century bestseller. He paid a friend a penny to hold his plough-horse whilst he walked to Stamford to buy it. From then on Clare's life would be one of secret journeys and long confinements, of a single moment of literary 'success' and many years of marvellous work whose greatness would not be understood until the 1960s. Extremes marked his existence. He kept company with gifted countrymen – and madmen. He became a caged bird and the singer of open fields. Due to a young Scottish schoolteacher seeking prospects along the Great North Road, he inherited distant ancestry. It was enough to cause him at times to see himself as another Robert Burns. Although his publishers promoted him as a second Robert Bloomfield. Confusions of all kinds brought mental illness and isolation. No-one knows where his genius came from, but it allowed him to put into words everything which an English countryman of his day saw and did.

To read John Clare is to enter a world which is both ordinary and yet beyond anything which 'history' can tell us. He wrote at a time when the factories were taking over the landworkers. Dubbed peasant-poet in his day, his voice has no equal in ours. There is a freshness and strength about it which excites us. It is as though we had never seen plants and birds before we read him. And although his own life was in so many ways appalling, his transcendence of its difficulties and hurts makes us love him. Not to have read John Clare is a huge loss. He is our best teacher when it comes to birds and flowers, and it is his sentiments which continue to protect our landscape. Nor can there be a more passionate defender of human nature in all its contours. He is an inexhaustible writer. We would not understand ourselves as we do had he not existed.

Ronald Blythe
President of the John Clare Society

~ Primula vulgaris ~

Primrose

'The pale brimstone primroses come at the spring,
Swept over and fann'd by the wild thrushes wing'
John Clare

'As a sweet pledge of Spring, the little lambs
Bleat in the varied weather round their dams
Or huge molehill, or Roman mound behind
Like spots of snow, lye sheltered from the wind

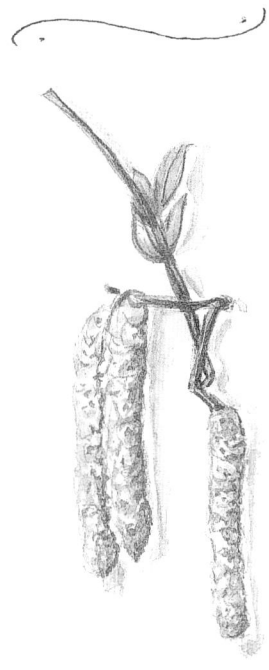

January

A Winters Day ~ from *Shepherd's Calendar*   22 ~ 23
Journal, 2nd January 1825   24
Winter Snowstorm, Poem   — 25
Journal 5th ~ 31st January 1825   26 ~ 27

February

The Thaw ~ from *Shepherd's Calendar*   28 ~ 29
~·· — ~·· ~ ~·· ~ ~·· — continued   30 ~ 31
From a letter written 7th Feby 1825   32 ~
Journal 4th Feby 1825   — 33
The Robin, from a letter March 6th 1825   34 ~
The Red Robin Poem   ~ 35
Some Days Before Spring Poem   36 ~ 37

March

The Insect World from *Shepherd's Calendar*   38 ~ 39
Journal 1st ~ 14th March 1825   40 —
The Droneing Bee Poem   — 41
I took a walk to botanise, from a letter Mar 25th 1825   42 ~ 43
The Nightingale, Prose   44 ~ 45
The Nightingale's Nest. Poem   45 ~ 47
On Birds and their Nests, Prose   48 — 49
The Yellow Hammer, Poem   48 ~
The Thrushe's Nest Poem   50 ~
The Hedge Sparrow Nest Poem   50 ~
March bids farewell, from *Shepherd's Calendar*   — 51
The Blackbird, Poem   52 —
The Whitethorn   Poem   ~ 53

JANUARY

Again the robin waxes tame,
And ventures pity's crumbs to claim,
Picking the trifles off the snow,
Which dames on purpose, daily throw;
And perching on the windowsill,
Where memory, recolecting still, ...

..... Knows the last winters broken pane,
And there he hops and peeps again,
The clouds of starnels daily fly
Blackening thro' the evening sky
To Whittlesea's reed~wooded mere,
And ozier holts by rivers near;
And many a mingl'd swathy crowd~
Rook, crow, and Jackdaw~noising loud,
Fly to and fro to dreary fen,
Dull winter's weary flight agen,
Flopping on heavy wings away
As soon as morning wakens grey,
And, when the sun sets round and red
Returns to naked woods to bed.
Wood~pigeons too, in flocks appear,
By hunger tam'd from timid fear
They, mid the sheep, unstart'ld steal
And share wi' them a scanty meal,
Picking the green leaves want bestows
Of turnips sprouting thro' the snows...

from Shepherd's Calendar. January

23

Sunday 2nd January 1825.

Received a parcel from Mrs. Emmerson. Took a walk to Simon's Wood:
found three distinct species of the bramble. Henderson will have it
there are but two but I am certain he is wrong, and believe there are
four, the common one that grows in the hedges, the larger sort that grows
on commons bearing large fruit called by the children 'black~berry' the
small creeping dewberry that runs along the ground in the land fur-
rows and on the brink of brooks, and a much larger one of the same kind
growing in woods. Botanists may say what they will; for though these
are all of a family they are distinctly different. There are two sorts of
the wild rose, the one in the hedges bearing blush~coloured flowers,
and the other much smaller in the woods with white ones.

The Journal 1824-25.

WINTER SNOWSTORM.

Winter is come in earnest, and the snow,
In dazzling splendour crumping underfoot,
Spreads a white world all calm, and where we go
By hedge or wood, trees shine from top to root
In feathered foliage, flashing light and shade
In strangest contrast; fancy's pliant eye
Delighted sees a vast romance displayed,
And fairy halls descended from the sky;
The smallest twig its snowy burthen bears,
The woods o'erhead the dullest eyes engage
To shape strange things, where arch and pillar bears
A roof of grains fantastic, arched and high;
A little shed beside the spinney wears
The grotesque semblance of an hermitage. ~

Wednesday 5th January 1825.

Gilliflowers, polyanthuses, marigold and the yellow-yarrow are in flower, and the double scarlet anemone nearly out, crocuses peeping out above the ground, swelling with flower.

The authoress [Elizabeth Kent] of the Flora Domestica says the snowdrop is the first Spring flower: she is mistaken: the yellow-aconite is always earlier, and the first on the list of Spring.

Friday 7th January.

Bought some cakes of colour: with the intention of trying to make sketches of curious snailhorns, butterflies, moths and sphinxes, wild flowers, and whatever my wanderings may meet with that are not too common.

Monday 31st January.

Went to Simon's Wood for a sucker of the barberry bush to set in my garden, saw the corn-tree putting out in leaf.

A yellow crocus and a bunch of snowdrops in full flower. The mavis thrush has been singing all day long.

Spring seems begun. The woodbine all over the wood are in full leaf.

from 'The Journal 1824 – 25

Hornet Moth   J.C.

February

The Thaw.

The snow, it's gone, from cottage tops,
   The thatch-moss glows in brighter green;
And eaves in quick succession drop,
   Where grinning icicles have been;
Pit~patting with a pleasant noise
   In tubs set by the cottage~door;
And ducks, and geese, wi happy joys,
   Douse in the yard~pond brimming o'er.

The sun peeps thro' the window-pane:
    Which children mark with laughing eye,
And in the wet street steal again,
    To tell each other Spring is nigh:
And as young hope the past recalls,
    In playing groups will often draw,
Building beside the sunny walls
    Their spring-play-huts of sticks or straw.

And oft in pleasure's dream they hie
    Round homesteads by the village side,
Scratching the hedgerow mosses bye,
    Where painted pooty shells abide,
Mistaking oft the ivy spray
    For leaves that come with budding Spring,
And wond'ring, in their search for play,
    Why birds delay to build and sing.

The milkmaid singing leaves her bed
    As glad as happy thoughts can be,
While magpies chatter o'er her head
    As jocund in the change as she:
Her cows around the closes stray,
    Nor ling'ring wait the foddering-boy;
Tossing the mole-hills in their play,
    And staring round with frolic joy.

Ploughmen go whistling to their toils,
    And yoke again the rested plough;
And, mingling o'er the mellow soils,
    Boys shout, and whips are noising now,
The shepherd now is often seen
    By warm banks o'er his hook to bend;
Or o'er a gate or stile to lean,
    Chattering to a passing friend.

Odd hive bees fancying winter is o'er,
    And dreaming in their combs of Spring;
Creeps on the slab beside their door
    And strokes its legs upon its wing:
While wild ones, half asleep, are humming
    Round snow-drop bells, a feeble note,
And pigeons coo of Summer coming,
    Picking their feathers on the cote......

Shepherd's Calendar 'February'

....A calm of pleasure listens round,
    And almost whispers, winter's bye;
While fancy dreams of summer sounds,
    And quiet rapture fills the eye,
The sun~beams on the hedges lye,
    The south wind murmers summer soft;
And maids hang out white cloaths to dry,
    Around the eldern skirted croft.

Each barn's green thatch reeks in the sun,
    It's mate, the happy sparrows calls,
And as nest building spring begun,
    Peeps in the holes about the walls:
The wren, a sunny~side the stack,
    Wi' short tail ever on the strunt,
Cock'd, gadding up above his back,
    Again for dancing gnats will hunt ....

...Hens leave their roosts wi' cackling calls,
    To see the barn door free from snow;
And cocks flye up the mossy walls
    To clap their spangled wings and crow;
About the steeples sunny top,
    The jackdaw flocks resemble spring,
And in the stone arch'd windows pop,
    Wi summer noise and wanton wing.

The small birds think their wants are o'er,
    To see the snow~hills, fret again,
And, from the barn's chaff~litter'd door,
    Betake them to the greening plain.
The woodman's robin startles coy,
    Nor longer at his elbow comes,
To peck, wi' hunger's eager joy,
    'Mong mossy stulps the litter'd crumbs.

'Neath hedge and walls that screen the wind,
　The gnats for play will flock together;
And e'en poor flyes odd hopes will find
　To venture in the mocking weather;
From out their hidy~holes again,
　Wi' feeble pace, they often creep
Along the sun~warm'd window~pane,
　Like dreaming things that walk in sleep.

The mavis thrush wi' wild delight,
　Upon the orchard's dripping tree,
Mutters, to see the day so bright,
　Spring scraps of young hope's poesy:
And of't dame stops her burring wheel
　To hear the robin's note once more,
That tuttles while he pecks his meal
　From sweet~briar hips beside the door.

The hedgehog, from his hollow root,
　Sees the wood~moss clear of snow,
And hunts each hedge for fallen fruit—
　Crab, hip, and winter~bitten sloe;
And oft, when check'd by sudden fears,
　As shepherd~dog his haunt espies
He rolls up in a ball of spears
　And all his barking rage defies.

Thus Nature of the Spring will dream
　While south winds thaw; but soon again
Frost breathes upon the stiffening stream,
　And numbs it into ice: the plain
Soon wears its merry garb of white;
　And icicles, that fret at noon,
Will eke their icy tails at night
　Beneath the chilly stars and moon....
　　　from. Shepherd's Calendar February.

31

I always think that this month, the prophet of Spring, brings many beauties to the landscape, though a careless observer would laugh at me for saying so, who believes that it brings nothing because he does not give himself the trouble to seek them.

I always admire the kindling freshness that the bark of different sorts of trees and underwood assumes in the forest; the 'foul royce' twigs kindling into a vivid colour at their tops, as red as pigeons claws; the Ash with its grey bark and black swelling buds; the Birch with its 'paper-rind'; and the darker, mottled sorts of Hazel; Black Alder with the greener hues of Sallow Willow; the bramble that still wears its leaves, with the privet of purple hue; while the straggling wood briar shines in a brighter and more beautiful green than leaves can boast at this season. Odd forward branches in the new~laid hedges of whitethorn begin to freshen into green before the arum dare peep out of its hood or the primrose and violet shoot up a new leaf through the warm moss and ivy that shelter their spring dwellings. The furze, too, on the common, wears a fairer green, and here and there an odd branch is covered with golden flowers.

The ling or heather nestling among the long grass below (covered with the withered flowers of last year) is sprouting up into fresh hopes of spring. The fairy rings on the pastures are getting deeper dyes, and the water-weeds, with long, silver~green blades of grass, are mantling the stagnant ponds in their summer liveries. In fact, I find more beauties in this month than I can find room to talk about.

Extract from a letter written on
7th Feb. 1825.

4ᵗʰ February . Friday.

The first winters day; a sharp frost and a nightfall of snow
drifted in heaps by a keen wind. There has been a deal of talk
about the forwardness of this season, but last season was not
much behind.
On the third of this month I found a hedge~sparrow's nest in
Billing's boxtrees before the window, with three eggs in it. I
looked again in March and found two young ones, pen~feathered,
starved to death. She laid again in the same nest and brought
off a fledged brood.

from The Journal 1824-25

THE ROBIN.

The little robin has begun his summer song in good earnest. He was singing at my chamber window this morning almost before daylight as he has done all the week, and at nightfall he comes regularly to his old plum tree and starts again.

There is a plaintiff sweetness in the song of this bird, that I am very fond of; it may be called an eternal song, for it is heard at intervals all the year round, and in Autumn, when the leaves are all fled from the trees there is a melancholy sweetness in it, that is very touching to my feelings. The Robin is one of the most familiar birds that a village landscape possesses and it is no-less beloved, for even the children leave its nest unmolested; but the Wren and Martin are held in the like veneration with a many people who will not suffer their nests to be destroyed.

The Robin seems to be fond of the company and haunts of man; it builds its' nest close to his cottage, in the hovel or outhouse thatch, or behind the wood~bine or sweet~briar in the garden wall, nor does it seem to care to make any secret of its dwelling where its only enemy is the cat to whom its confidence of safety often falls prey, and it seeks food by his door or the dunghill or on the garden beds, nay it will even settle on the gardener's spade when he is at work to watch the worm that he throws up and un-bares, and in the winter it will venture into the house for food and becomes as tame as a chicken. We had one that used to come in at a broken pane in the window three winters together, I always knew it to be our old vis-itor by a white scar on one of the wings which might have been an old wound made by some cat, it grew so tame that it would perch on ones finger and take crumbs out of the hand, it was very much startled by the cat at first but after a time it took little notice of her further then always contriving to keep out of her way, it would never stay in the house at night, tho' it would attempt to perch on the chair spindles and clean its bill and ruffle its feathers and put its head under it's wing as if it had made up it's mind to stay, but something or other always molest-ed it when suddenly sought its old broken pane and depart; it has been a com-mon notion among heed-less observers that the rob-in frequents nowhere but in villages, but this is an erronious one, for it is found in the deepest sol-itudes of the woods and forests, where it lives on in-seeks and builds it's nest on the roots or stools

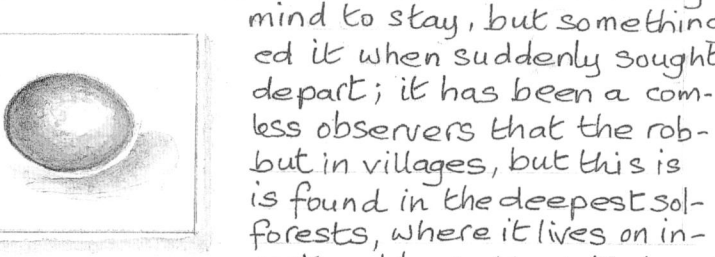

of the underwood or a hanging bank by a dykeside which is often mistook for that of the nightingales. I have often observed its fond-ness for man even here, for in summer I scarcley cross a wood but a Robin suddenly falls in my path to court my acquaintance and pay me a visit where it hops and flutters about as if pleased to see me, and in Winter it is the woodmans companion for the whole day and whole season......it is not commonly known that the Robin is a very quar-relsome bird, it is not only at frequent warfare with its own species, but attacks boldley every other small bird that comes in its way and is gen-erally the conqueror, I have seen it chase the housesparrow, which is a very pert bird, never ventures to fight it, linnets and finches that crowd the barn doors in winter never stands against its authority, but flyes from its in-terferences and acknowledge it the 'Cock~of~the~walk' and he always seems to consider the right of the yard as his own.

From Natural History Letters 1825-27

21st February. Monday. 1825.
A robin busy at building it's nest in the garden.

THE RED ROBIN.

Cock Robin he had a neat tippet at Spring,
And he sat in a shed and heard other birds sing,
And he whistled a ballad, as loud as he could,
And built him a nest of oak leaves by the wood.

And furnished it just as the celandine pressed,
Like a bright burning blaze by the edge of its nest,
All glittering with sunshine and beautiful rays,
Like high polished brass or the fire in a blaze.

Then sung a new song on the bend o' the brere,
And so it kept singing the whole of the year,
Till cowslips and wild roses blossomed and died,
The red Robin sung, by the old Spring side.

Some Days Before the Spring.

There's a gladness of heart in the first days of Spring
There's a pleasure in memory to hear the birds sing,
The Pink or Hedgesparrow will sing at daybreak
Thou a leaf on the hedges is hardly awake
As for flowers on the grass there's not one to be seen
And the grass in the fields scarce enough to be green
The ruts full of water all muddy and thick
Which the boy tries to stop with a bit of a stick.

The bits of brown haystacks all cut to the core
In the grassy close corners show winter is o'er
With the oaks frowning o'er them all mossy and grey
They will stand in the shelter 'till they cut the new hay
The fieldfare is there a seeking hedge fruits
And the crow on the grass, is boreing for roots
With the jackdaw that nauntles among the molehills
In their grey powdered wigs, and bright yellow bills....

The stones in the brooks, are all covered with green
All trailing and spreading as mosses are seen
In the woods at the spring and the close of the year
When violets and primroses like sisters appear
How level the meadow, how saffron the sun
How fine is the web that the spider has spun
Round twigs of the hedge and bents of the vales
In the soft mornings sunshine and sweet evenings gales

~

Then come let us walk and enjoy the brisk air
And fancy the change when sweet spring it is there
Wild flowers in the grass, and nests in the trees
A hedge for the birds and a flower for the bees
So away let us walk while the suns in the sky
And the paths o'er the greensward and rushes are dry
And Mary will see what there is to be seen
The hedges swelled buds, and the meadows more green.

March

...The insect-world, now sunbeams higher climb,
Oft dream of Spring, and wake before their time.
Blue flyes from straw stack, crawling scarce alive,
And bees peep out on slabs before the hive,
Stroaking their little legs across their wings,
And venturing short flight where the snow-drop hings
Its silver bell ~ and winter aconite
Wi' buttercup ~ like flowers that shut at night,
And green leaf frilling round their cups of gold,
Like tender maiden muffled from the cold:
They sip, and find their honey ~ dreams are vain,
And feebly hasten to their hives again.—
And butterflys, by eager hopes undone,
Glad as a child come out to greet the sun,
Lost, neath the shadow of a sudden shower,
Nor left to see tomorrow's April flower.....
        from 'Shepherd's Calendar March

Snowdrop   Galanthus nivalis
Winter Aconite   Eranthis hyemalis

Tuesday 1st March. 1825.

Saw today the largest piece of ivy I ever saw in my life, mailing a tree which it nearly surpassed in size in Oxey Wood. It was thicker than my thigh and it's cramping embraces seemed to diminish the tree to a dwarf. It has been asserted by some that ivy is very injurious to trees and by others that it does no injury at all. I cannot decide against it. The large pieces were covered all over with root~like fibres as thick as hair, and they represented the limbs on animals more than the bark of a tree.

Wednesday 7th March.

The birds were singing in Oxey Wood at six o'clock this evening as loud and as various as in May.

Monday 14th March.

My double scarlet anemone in flower. A sharp frosty morning.

Monday 21st March.

Had a double polyanthus and a single white hepatica sent me from Stamford, round which was wrapped a curious prospectus of an *Every Day Book*, by W. Hone. If such a thing were well got up it would make one of the most entertaining things ever published; and I think the prospectus bids fair to do something. There is a fine quotation from Herrick for a motto. How delightful is the freshness of these old poets; It is like meeting with green spots in desserts.

From The Journal

The Droneing Bee.

The droneing bee has wakened up,
And humming round the buttercup;
Around the bright star daisy hums ; —
O'er every blade of grass he passes —
The dew~drop shines like looking glasses;
In every drop a bright sun comes : ——
Tis March, and Spring, bright days we see, —
'Round every blossom hums the bee.

As soon as daylight in the morning,
The crimson curtains of the dawning, —
We hear, and see, the humming bee, —
Searching for hedge~row violets,
Happy with the food he gets : ——
Swimming o'er brook, and meadow lea;—
He sits on maple stools at rest,
On the green mosses velvet breast.

About the molehill, round, and round,
The wild bees hums with honied sound,—
Singing a song, of spring, and flowers, —
To school~boys heard in sunny hours.
When all the waters seem a blaze,
Of fire and sunshine in such days;
When bee's buzz on with coal~black eye;
Joined by the yellow butterfly.

And when it comes, a summer shower:
It still will go from flower, to flower;
Then underneath the rushes, —
It sees the silver daisy flower,
And there it spends a little hour.
Then hides among the bushes.
But whence they come from, where they go
None but the wiser schoolboys know.

March 25th 1825.

I took a walk today to botanise and found that the Spring had
taken up her dwelling in good earnest. She has covered the woods
with white anemonie, which the children call ladysmocks and the
hare~bells are just venturing to unfold their blue dropping bells,
the green is covered with daisies and the little celandine; the
hedge bottoms are crowded with green leaves of the arum, where
the boy is peeping for pooties with eager anticipations and delight.
The sallows are cloathed in their golden palms, where the bees
are singing a busy welcome to spring, they seem uncommonly
fond of these flowers and gather around them in swarms. I
have often wondered how these little travellers found their way
home again from the woods and solitudes where they journey for
wax and honey. I have seen them today, at least 3 miles from any
village, in Langley Wood, working at their palms and some of them
with their little thighs so loaded with the yellow dust as to seem
almost unable to flye. It is curious to see how they collect their
load; they keep wiping their legs over their faces, to gather the
dust that settles there after creeping in the flowers, till
they have got a sufficient load and then they flye home~ward
to their hives. I have heard that a man curious to know how far
his bees travelled in a summer's day, got up early one morning
and stood by one of his hives to powder them as they came out
with fine flour to know them again.... and having to go to the mar~
ket that day he passed by a turnip field, in full flower, about 5
miles from home and to his surprise, he found some of his own in
their white powdered coats busily humming at their labour with
the rest. ～～

The ivy berries are quite ripe and the Wood~pigeons are busily fluskering among the ivy dotterels on the skirts of the common .... have you never heard that cronking jarring noise in the woods at this early season? I heard it today and went into the woods to examine what thing it was that caused the sound and discovered that it was the common green woodpecker busily employed at boring his hole which he effected by twisting his bill around in the way that a carpenter twists his wimble, with this difference, that when he has got it to a certain extent, he turns it back then pecks a while and then twists agen, his beak seems to serve all the purposes of a nail~ passer, gough, and wimble effectually.

From Natural History Letters 1825 - 37

I went to take my walk today and heard the Nightingale for the first time this season in Royce Wood just at the town end. We may now be assured that summer is nigh at hand; you asked me a long while back to procure you a Nightingale's nest and eggs and I have try'd every season since to find if the bird-nesting boys have ever taken one out, but I have not been able to procure one; when I was a boy I used to be very curious to watch the nightingale to find her nest and to observe her colour and size, for I had heard many odd tales about her and often observed her habits and found her nest, so I shall be able to give you a pretty faithfull history ~ she is a plain bird, something like the hedge~sparrow in shape and the female Firetail or Redstart in colour, but more slender than the former and of a redder brown or scorched colour then the latter, the breast of the male or female is spotted, like a young Robin, and the feathers on the rump and on parts of the wing are of a fox~red or burnt~umber hue, one of them is of a darker brown then the other but I know not whether it be the male or female, they gener~ally seek the same solitudes which they haunted last season and these are the black~thorn clumps and thickets about the woods and spinneys, they sit in the water~grains of oaks or on a twig of hazel and sing their varied songs with short intervals bothin the night and day time and sing in one as common as the other, I have watched them often at their song, their mouths are open very wide and th~eir feathers are ruffled up and their wings trembling, as if in extacy, the sup~erstition of laying their throats on a sharp thorn is foolish absurdity, but it is not the only one ascribed to the nightingale: they make a large nest of the old leaves, that strew the ground in woods and green moss and line it with hair and sometimes with a little fine with'rd grass or wool, it is a very deep nest

and is generally placed on the root or stub of a black or white thorn, sometimes a little height up the bush and often on the ground, they lay 5 eggs about the size of the wood~ larks, or larger, and of a deep olive~brown without spot or tinge of another colour, their eggs have a very odd appearance and are unlike any other birds in the country, when they have young their song ceases and they make an odd burring noise as if call~ ing their young to their food, they are very jealous of intrusions on their privacy when they have young and if one goes into their haunts at that time, they make a great chirring and burring and will almost perch close to you, noising and chirping, as if to frighten you away, at first one assails you and after it has been chirping about you a while the ot~ her approaches to join it, but as soon as you get a little distance from the haunts, they leave you and

are still, when, if you return, they resume their former chirping and con-
tinue fluttering about you among the branches till you leave them agen
to their privacy.
Their nests are very difficult to find, indeed it is a hopeless task to hunt
for them as they are seldom found but by accident being hidden among the
tall weeds that surround the roots and cover the woods undisturbed rec-
-esses. When I was a boy I found three nests one season and all were fo-
und by chance in crossing the woods hunting the nests of other birds, the
Redbreast frequently builds on the ground under the shelter of a knoll
or stulp and its nest is often taken for that of the nightingales, but it is
easily distinguished from it as the robins is built with dead grass and moss
on the outside while the Nightingale never forgets the dead oak leaves and
this is so peculiar to her taste that I never saw a nest of theirs without
them, nor are they used by any other bird for their nests,

[The Nightingale] April 21ˢᵗ 1825.

The Nightingales Nest.

Up this green woodland ride let's softly rove,
And list the nightingale ~ she dwelleth here
Hush! let the wood gate softly clap - for fear
The noise may drive her from her home of love;
For here I've heard her many a merry year —
At morn, at eve, nay, all the live long day,
As though she lived on song this very spot,
Just where that old~man's beard all wildly trails
Rude arbours o'er the road, and stops the way ~
And where that child its blue~bell flowers hath got,
Laughing and creeping through the mossy rails.
There have I hunted like a very boy,
Creeping on hands and knees through matted thorn
To find her nest, and see her feed her young.
And vainly did I many hours employ:
All seemed as hidden as a thought unborn.
And where these crimping fern-leaves ramp among ......
The hazel's under boughs,

Cont....

......The hazel's under boughs, I've nestled down,
And watched her while she sung; and her renown
Hath made me marvel that so famed a bird
Should have no better dress than russet brown.
Her wings would tremble in her extacy
And feathers stand on end, as 'twere with joy,
And mouth wide open to release her heart
Of its out sobbing songs. The happiest part
Of summer's fame she shared, for so to me
Did happy fancys shapen her employ;
But if I touched a bush, or scarcely stirred,
All in a moment stopt. I watched in vain:
The timid bird had left the hazel bush,
And at a distance hid to sing again.
Lost in a wilderness of listening leaves,
Rich extacy would pour it's luscious strain,
Till envy spurred the emulating thrush
To start less wild and scarce inferior songs;
For cares with him for half the year remain,
To damp the ardour of his speckled breast;
The nightingales to summer's life belongs,
And naked trees, and winter's nipping wrongs,
Are strangers to her music and her rest.
Her joys are evergreen, her world is wide
— Hark! there she is as usual — let's be hush —
For in this black-thorn clump, if rightly guessed,
Her curious house is hidden. Part aside
These hazel branches in a gentle way,
And stoop right cautious 'neath the rustling boughs,
For we will have another search today,
And hunt this fern-strewn thorn-clump round and round;
And where this seeded wood-grass idly bows,
We'll wade right through, it is a likely nook:
In such like spots, and often on the ground,
They'll build, where rude boys never think to look —
Aye, as I live! her secret nest is here,
Upon this white-thorn stump! I've searched about
For hours in vain. There! put that bramble by —
Nay, trample on its branches and get near.

— How subtle is the bird! she started out,
And raised a plaintive note of danger nigh,
Ere we were past the brambles; and now, near
Her nest, she sudden stops - as choking fear,
That might betray her home. So even now
We'll leave it as we found it: safety's guard
Of pathless solitudes shall keep it still.
See there! she's sitting on the old oak bough,
Mute in her fears; our presence doth retard
Her joys, and doubt turns every rapture chill.
— Sing on, sweet bird! may no worse hap befall
Thy visions, then the fear that now deceives.
We will not plunder music of its dower,
Nor turn this spot of happiness to thrall
For melody seems hid in every flower,
That blossoms near thy home. Those harebells all
Seem bowing with the beautiful in song;
And gaping cuckoo~pint, with spotted leaves,
Seems blushing of the singing it has heard.
How curious is the nest; no other bird
Uses such loose materials, or weaves
It's dwelling in such spots: dead oaken leaves
Are placed without, and velvet moss within,
And little scraps of grass, and, scant and spare,
Of what seems scarce materials, down, and hair;
For from men's haunts she seemeth nought to win.
Yet Nature is the builder, and contrives
Homes for her children's comfort, even here;
Where solitude's disciples spend their lives
Unseen, save when a wanderer passes near
That loves such pleasant places. Deep adown,
The nest is made a hermit's mossy cell.
Snug lie her curious eggs, in number, five,
Of deadened green, or rather olive brown;
And the old prickly thorn~bush guards them well.
And here we'll leave them, still unknown to wrong,
As the old woodland's legacy of song.

From, The Rural Muse, 1835.

47

Hedgesparrow.

On Birds and Their Nests.

I have often wondered how birds nests escape injuries which are built upon the ground. I have found larks nests in an old cart-rut, grassed over, and pettichaps close on the edge of a horse track in a narrow lane where two carts could not pass and two oxen would even have difficulty in doing so, but yet, I never found a nest destroyed, providence, was their protector and on the cow pasture I have often seen an hungry ox sturt his head on one side making a snufting noise and cease eating for a minute or two and then turn in another direction, and on going to see what it turned from, I have started up the old bird and found its nest by this sign.

The nightingales nest in the orchard hedge, was composed with ~out side of maple leaves and some oak leaves and lined within, with withered grass and a few fragments of oak leaves.

Bullfinch

Skylark

Goldfinch

The Yellowhammer.

When shall I see the white-thorn leaves agen,
And Yellowhammers gath'ring the dry bents
By the dyke side, on stilly moor or fen,
Feathered wi love and natures good intents.
Rude is the nest this Architect invents,
Rural the place, wi cart ruts by dyke side.
Dead grass, horsehair, and downy headed bents
Tied to dead thistles she doth well provide,
Close to a hill o'ants where cowslips bloom
And shed o'er meadows far their sweet perfume.
In early Spring, when winds blow chilly cold,
The Yellowhammer, trailing grass, will come
To fix a place and choose an early home,
With yellow breast and head of solid gold.

Yellow-hammer

Whitethroat

Furze-linnet

Long-tailed
Titmouse

Chaffinch.

Long-tailed titmouse, chaffinch and redcap, make a most beautiful
outside to their nests of grey lichen; linnets and hedgesparrows make
a loose ruff outside of coarse green moss, wool and roots, the first are
like the freestone fabrics of finished ellegance, the latter like the rough
plain walls of a husbandman's cottage, yet, equally warm and comfort-
able within. Pinks use cowhair and some feathers for their inside hang-
ings, red-caps get thistledown, hedgesparrows use wool and cowhair
intermixed, linnets use wool and cowhair and the Furze-linnet uses
rabbit down. These four sorts of birds never (I think) are known to use
horse hair and this universaly. Bullfinches make a slight nest of
sticks and small roots, very shallow. White-throats use dead harrif
stalks linked with cobwebs and lined with fine roots and horse hair.

From Natural History Letters 1825 - 37

The Thrushes Nest.

Within a thick and spreading 'awthorn bush,
That overhung a molehill large and round,
I heard from morn to morn a merry thrush
Sing hymns to sunrise, while I drank the sound
With joy; and, often an intruding guest
I watched her secret toil from day to day –
How true she warped the moss, to form her nest,
And modelled it within with wood and clay;
And bye and bye, like heath-bells gilt with dew,
There lay her shining eggs, as bright as flowers,
Ink-spotted-over shells of greeny blue;
And there I witnessed in the summer hours
A brood of nature's minstrels chirp and fly,
Glad as the sunshine and laughing sky.

The Hedge~Sparrow

The tame hedge-sparrow, in its russet dress,
Is half a robin for its gentle ways,
And, the bird loving dame, can do no less
Then throw it out a crumble on cold days.
In early March it into garden strays,
And in the snug clipt box-tree green and round,
It makes a nest of moss, and hair, and lays
When een the snow, is lurking on the ground.
It's eggs in number five of greenish blue,
Bright, beautiful, and glossy shining shells,
Much like the fire~tail's, but of a brighter hue.
Yet in her garden home much danger dwells,
Where skulking cat with mischief in its breast,
Catches their young before they leave the nest.

......March bids farewell, wi garlands in her hair
Of hazzel tassles, woodbine's hairy sprout,
And sloe and wild-plum blossoms peeping out
In thickest knotts of flowers, preparing gay,
For April's reign, a mockery of May.
            'Shepherd's Calendar 'March'

The Blackbird.

The blackbird is a bonny bird
    That singeth in the wood
His song is in the evening heard
    When the red cow chews her cud
His song is heard in morning loud
    Upon the bright white thorn
While the blythe milkmaid sings as proud
    And the world in scorn

Oh bonny is the blackbird still
    On top of yon fir tree
On which he wipes his golden bill
    And blithely whistles he
He sings upon the sapling oak
    In notes all rich and mellow
Oft have I quit towns noise, and folk
    In Springs sweet summer weather.

The blackbird is a bonny bird
    I love his mourning suit
And song in the spring mornings heard
    As mellow as the flute.
How sweet his song in April showers
    Pipes from his golden bill
As yellow as the kingcup flowers
    The sweetest ditty still.

How beautiful the White-thorn shows its leaves
The first in Springs beginnings, March or close
Of April, how very green it weaves
The branches in the underwood, they burst
More green than grass the common eye receives
Pleasures o'er green White thorn clumps in the wood
So beautifully green it seems at first
It does the eye that gazes on it good
The green enthusiasm of young Spring
The blackbird chooses it from all the wood
With moss to build his early nest and sing
Among the leaves the young are snugly nurst
Mornings young dew wets each pin-feathered wing
Before a bunch of May was from its white knobs burst.

~Dog Rose~

~Hedge Rose~

Rosa Canina

....The Dog Rose near the oak tree grew,
Blush'd swelling 'neath a veil of dew...
John Clare.

......'Thrice welcome sweet Summer in softness returning,
Thrice welcome ye skies wi' no clouds on your brow'.....

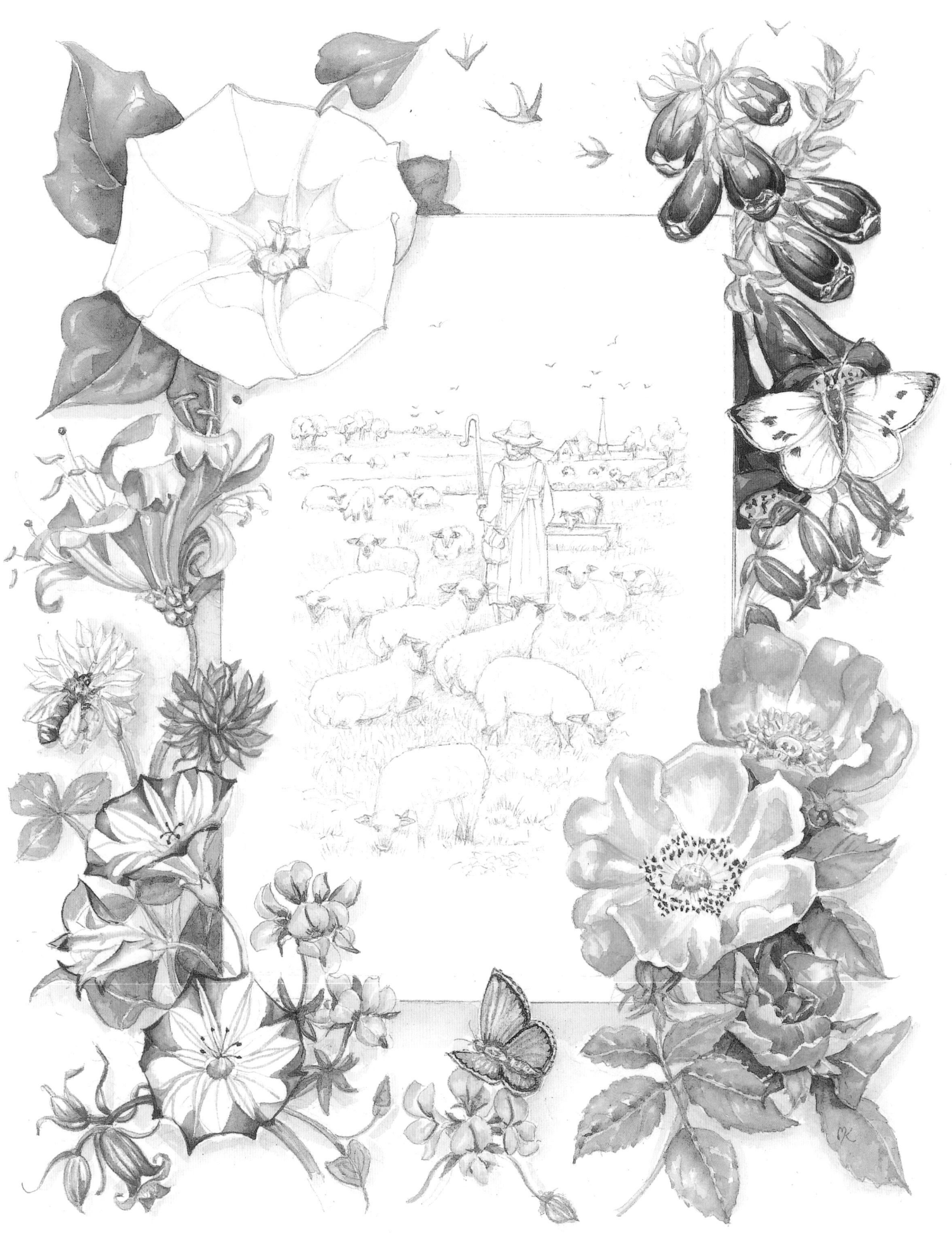

April

The infant April from Shepherd's Calendar   58 ~ 59
The Journal 14th ~ 18th April 1825   60 ~ 61
Primroses   Poem   62 ~ 63
The dewdrops on every blade of grass. Prose   64 ~
The Wren   Poem   ~ 65
The Anemone Poem   66 ~ 67
The Violet   ~"~   68 ~ 69

May.

The Bluebells too, from Shepherd's Calendar   70 ~ 71
   ~"~   ~"~   continued   72 ~
The Journal 16th ~ 19th May 1825   ~ 73
I Love Wild Flowers   Poem   74 ~ 75
   ~"~   ~"~   Illustration   76 ~ 77
The Crab Tree   78 ~
The Journal   26th May   ~ 79
The Red~bagged Bee   Poem   80 ~
The Journal   28th May   ~ 81
Clock ~ a ~ Clay   Poem   82 ~ 83

June

Now Summer is in Flower, from Shepherd's Calendar 84 ~ 85
The wheat swells into ear   ~"~   ~"~   ~"~   86 ~ 87
Now when sheering of the flocks   ~"~   ~"~   88 - 89
And London tufts   ~"~   ~"~   90 - 91
And White and Purple Jilliflowers etc ~"~   ~"~   92 - 93
Mong their old Wild companions etc   ~"~   ~"~   94 - 95
The Journal 3rd ~ 21st June 1825   96 - 97

April

The infant April joins the Spring,
  And views it's watery sky,
As youngling linnet tryes its wing,
  And fears at first to flye
With timid step she ventures on,
  And hardly dares to smile,
The blossoms open one by one,
  And sunny hours beguile.

But finer days approacheth yet,
  With scenes more sweet to charm,
And suns arrive that rise and set
  Bright strangers to a storm:
And, as the birds, with louder song,
  Each morning's glory cheers,
With bolder step she speeds along,
  And looses all her fears.

....In wanton gambols, like a child,
   She tends her early toils,
And seeks the buds along the wild,
   That blossom while she smiles;
And laughing on, with nought to chide,
   She races with the hours,
Or sports by Nature's lovely side,
   And fills her lap with flowers.

Tho, at her birth, north cutting gales
   Her beautys oft disguise,
And hopefull blossoms turning, pales,
   Upon her bosom dies;
Yet ere she seeks another place
   And ends her reign in this,
She leaves us with as fair a face
   As ere gave birth to bliss.

And fairy month of waking mirth
   From whom our joys ensue,
Thou early gladder of the earth
   Thrice welcome here anew;
With thee the bud unfolds to leaves
   The grass greens on the lea,
And flowers their tender boon receives
   To bloom and smile with thee.

The shepherds on his pasture walks
   The first fair cows-lip finds,
Whose tufted flowers, on tender stalks,
   Keep nodding to the winds,
And tho thy thorns withold the May,
   Their shades the violets bring,
Which children stoop for in their play
   As tokens of the Spring.....

from Shepherd's Calendar April.

14th April. Thursday 1825.

The snakehead or fritillary in flower; also the light blue, pink and white hyacinths; bluebell, or harebell in flower; the primrose, violet and bedlam cowslip fading out of flower.

16th April. Saturday. Took a walk in the fields, bird-nesting and botanizing, and had like to have been taken up as a poacher in Hilly Wood, by a meddlesome, conceited keeper belonging to Sir John Trollop. He swore that he had seen me in act, more than once, of shooting game, when I never shot even so much as a sparrow in my life. What terrifying rascals these wood keepers and game keepers are! They make a prison of the forests and are its gaolors.

23rd April. Saturday. Saw the red-start or firetail today and the little willow wren. The blackthorn tree in full flower that shines about the hedges like cloaks out to dry.

28th April. Thursday. Hedge-sparrow finished her nest in Billing's box-tree and laid one egg. Walnut showing leaf: sycamore and horse-chestnut nearly covered. I observed a snail on his journey at full speed, and I marked by my watch that he went thirteen inches in three minutes, which was the utmost he could do without stopping to wind or rest. It was a large garden snail.

29th April. Friday. The Hedge-sparrow in the box-tree has been about twelve days building her nest, the robin in the wall about fourteen, and the jenny-wren near three weeks. Heard all through last night the sort of watch-ticking noise called a death watch. I observed there was one on each side of the chamber, and as soon as one finished ticking the other began: I think it is a call that the male and female use in the time of cohabiting.

From 'The Journal 1825 -37

Snake'shead Fritillary
  Fritillaria meleagris

Harebell
  Campanula rotundifolia

Hyacinth.

61

PRIMROSES.

I love the rath primroses, pale brimstone primroses,
   That bloom in thick wood and in the green closes;
I love the primroses whenever they come,
   Where the blue-fly sits pensive and the humble bees hum.
The pale brimstone primroses come at the spring,
   Swept over and fann'd by the wild thrushes wing,
Bow'd down to the leaf cover'd ground by the bees,
   Who sing their ballads thro' bushes and trees.

Like patches o' flame 'i' the ivy so green,
   And dark green oak leaves where the Autumn has been,
Put on thy straw-hat love and russet stuff gown,
   And see the pale primroses grow up and down,
The pale brimstone primroses, wild wood primroses,
   Which maids 'i' the dark woods make into posies:
Put on thy stuff gown love and off let us be,
   To seek brimstone primroses neath the oak tree.

Spring time is come love, primroses bloom fair,
   The sun o' the morning shines in thy bright hair,
The ancient wood shadows are bonny dark green
   That throw out like giants the stoven between,
While brimstone primroses like patches o' flame,
   Blaze through the dead leaves making ivy look tame
I love the rath primroses in hedgerows and closes
   Together let's wander to gather primroses.

The dew~drops on every blade of grass, are so much like silver drops, that I am obliged to stoop down as I walk, to see if they are pearls; and those sprinkled on the ivy~woven beds of primroses, underneath the hazels, whitethorn and maples, are so like gold beads, that I stooped down to feel if they were hard, but they melted from my fingers, and where the dew lies on the primroses, the violets and the whitethorn leaves, they are emerald and beryl, yet it is nothing more than the dews of the morning on the budding leaves; nay the road grasses are covered with gold and silver beads, and the further we go, the brighter they seem to shine like gold and silver; it is nothing more than the suns light and shade upon them in the dewy morning; every thorn point and every bramble spear has its trembling ornament; till the wind gets a little brisker and then all is shaken off and all the shining jewelry passes away into a common Spring morning, full of budding leaves, primroses, violets and vernal speedwell, bluebell and orchis and common place objects.

From 'Natural History Letters 1825 - 37

The Wren

Why is the cuckoo's melody preferred
And nightingale's sick song so madly praised
In poets rhymes? is there no other bird
In nature's minstrelsy that hath not raised
One's heart to extacy and mirth as well?
I judge not how another's taste is caught:
With mine, there's other birds that bear the bell
Whose song hath crowds of happy memorys brought.
Such is the robin singing in the dell
And the little wren that many a time hath sought
Shelter from showers in huts where I did dwell
At early spring the tenant of the plain
Keeping my sheep and still they come to tell
The happy storys of the past again..

~Anemone ranunculoides~

~Anemone nemorosa~

~Wood Anemone~

~Yellow Anemone~

WOOD ANEMONIE

The wood anemonie through dead oak leaves
And in the thickest woods now blooms anew,
And where the green briar and the brambles weaves
Thick clumps o'green anemonies thicker grew.
And weeping flowers in thousands pearl in dew
People the woods and brakes hid hollows there,
White, yellow and purpled hued the wide wood through;
What pretty, drooping, weeping flowers they are
The clip't frilled leaves, the slender stalks they bear
On which the drooping flower hangs weeping dew.
How beautiful, through April time and May
The woods look filled with wild anemonie,
And every little spinney now looks gay
With flowers, mid brushwood and the huge oak tree.

To the Violet.

Hail to the violet! Sweet careless spread
    Neath each warm bush and covert budding hedge.
In many a pleasing walk have I been led
    To seek thee~ promise of Spring's earliest pledge~
In modest coyness hanging down its head,
    Unconscious hiding beauties from the eye
And sweetly brooding o'er its graceful form,
    Shunning each vulgar gaze that saunters by
And tim'ly stooping from an April storm;
    As virtue startled by approaching harm
Shrinks from delusion's false betraying hand
    With bashful look that more the bosom warms.
So sweetest blossom the coy violet stands
    Tempting the plunderer with a double charm.

Come, Queen of Months! in company
With all thy merry minstrelsy:—
The restless cuckoo, absent long,
And twittering swallows' chimney~song;
And hedgerow crickets' notes, that run
From every bank that fronts the sun;
And swarthy bees, about the grass,
That stops wi' every bloom they pass,
And every minute, every hour,
Keep teazing weeds that wear a flower;
And Toil, and Childhood's humming joys!
For there is music in the noise......

The blue~bells too, that thickly bloom
Where man was never known to come;
And smell-smocks, that from the view retires
Mong rustling leaves and bowing briars;
And stooping lilies~of~the~valley,
That love with shades and dews todally
And bending, droop, on slender threads,
With broad hood-leaves above their heads,
Like white~robed maids, in summer hours,
Beneath umbrellas, shunning showers;—
These, from the bark-mens crushing treads
Oft perish in their blooming beds.
Stripp'd of its boughs and bark, in white
The trunk shines in the mellow light,
Beneath the green surviving trees,
That wave above it in the breeze,
And, waking whispers, slowly bend
As if they mourn'd their fallen friend.....

From Shepherd's Calendar 'May'

.....And scarlet-starry points of flowers,
    Pimpernel, dreading nights and showers,
    Oft call'd "the Shepherd's Weather-glass",
    That sleeps till suns have dried the grass,
    Then wakes, and spreads its creeping bloom
    Till clouds with threatening shadows come —
    Then close it shuts to sleep again:
    Which weeders see, and talk of rain;
    And boys, that mark them shut so soon,
    Call them "John that goes to bed at noon:"
    And fumitory too — a name
    That Superstition holds to fame —
    Whose red and purple mottled flowers
    Are cropp'd by maids in weeding hours,
    To boil in water, milk, and whey,
    For washes on a holiday,
    To make their beauty fair and sleek,
    And scare the tan from Summer's cheek;
    And simple small "Forget-me-not,"
    Eyed with a pin's-head yellow spot
    I' the middle of its tender blue,
    That gains from poets notice due:—
    These flowers, that toil by crowds destroys,
    Robbing them of their lowly joys,
    Had met the May with hopes as sweet
    As those her suns in gardens meet;
    And oft the dame will feel inclined,
    As childhood's memory comes to mind,
    To turn her hook away, and spare
    The blooms it loved to gather there!
    My wild field catalogue of flowers,
    Grows in my rhymes as thick as showers,
    Tedious and long as they may be,
    To some, they never weary me .....

                        from Shepherd's Calendar. May.

6th May. 1825. Friday.
Could not sleep at night. Got up at three o'clock in the morning
and walked about the fields. The birds were high in their songs in
Royce Wood and almost deafening. I heard the cricket~bird again
in full cry in Royce Wood; it is just like a child's 'screecher'.
Saw a hawk~like bird that made an odd noise like one of the
nightingale as if to decoy his prey into sight.

10th May 1825 Tuesday.
Saw a male and female of the tree~sparrow (as I suppose them) in
Royce Close hedge next the lane. The cockbird had a very black head,
and its shades of brown were more deep and distinct than the
house~sparrow. The female, when flying, showed two white feathers
in her tail. They seemed to have a nest in the hedgerow but I couldn't
find it. Saw pettichap in Bushy Close. Its note is more like 'chippi~
chap; it keeps in continual motion on the tops of trees, uttering
its note.

13th May 1825. Friday.
Met with an extraordinary incident today, while walking in Open
Wood to hunt a nightingale's nest. I pop't unawares on an old
fox and her four young cubs that were playing about. She saw me
and instantly approached me growling like an angry dog. I had
no stick, and tried all I could to fright her by imitating the bark
of a fox~hound, which only irratated her the more, and if I
had not retreated a few paces back she would have seized me:
when I set up an hallo she started.

                                   The Journal 1824~25

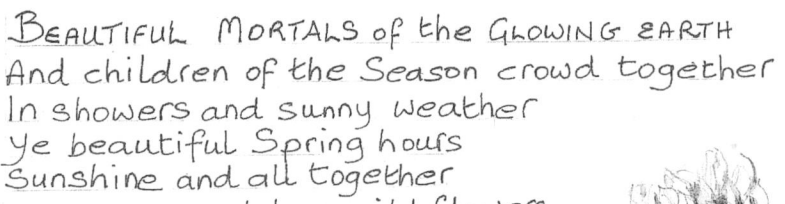

WILD FLOWERS

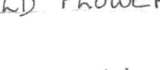

BEAUTIFUL MORTALS of the GLOWING EARTH
And children of the Season crowd together
In showers and sunny weather
Ye beautiful Spring hours
Sunshine and all together
                    I love wild flowers

The raindrops lodge on the swallows wing
Then fall on the meadow flowers
Cowslips and anemonies all come with spring
Beaded with first showers
The skylarks in the cowslips sing
                    I love wild flowers

Bluebells and cuckoo's in the wood
And pasture cuckoo's too
Red, yellow, white and blue
Growing where herd cows meet the showers
And lick the morning dew
                    I love wild flowers

The lakes and rivers ~ summer hours
All have their bloom as well
But few of these are childrens flowers
They grow where dangers dwell
In sun and shade and showers
                    I love wild flowers

They are such lovely things
And make the very seasons where they come
The nightingale is smothered where she sings
Above their scented bloom
O' what delight the cuckoo music brings
                    I love wild flowers.

1. Cowslip — *Primula veris*
2. Lady's smock — *Cardamine pratensis*
3. Snake'shead fritillary — *Fritillaria meleagris*
4. Wild Daffodil — *Narcissus pseudonarcissus*
5. Lesser Celandine — *Ranunculus ficaria*
6. Bluebell — *Endymion non-scriptus*
7. Wood Anemone — *Anemone nemorosa*
8. Common Dog Violet — *Viola riviniana*
9. Sweet Violet — *Viola odorata*
10. Lesser Periwinkle — *Vinca minor*
11. Primrose — *Primula vulgaris*
12. Bitter Vetchling — *Lathyrus montanus.*

a. Brimstone Butterfly — *Gonepteryx rhamni*

BEAUTIFUL MORTALS of the GLOWING EARTH

Plants of the Meadows and Woods
that flower in April and May.

The Crab Tree

Spring comes anew and brings each little pledge,
That still as wont my childish heart deceives,
I stoop again for violets in the hedge,
Among the ivy, and old withered leaves;
And often mark amid the clumps of sedge,
The pooty shells I gathered when a boy:
But cares have claimed me many an evil day,
And chilled the relish which I had for joy;
Yet, when crab blossoms blush among the may,
As wont in years gone bye I scramble now,
Up mid the brambles for my old esteems,
Filling my hands with many a blooming bough,
Till the heart stirring past, as present seems,
Save the bright sunshine, of those fairy dreams.

Took up my hyacinth bulbs and laid them in ridges of earth today.
Made a new frame for my auriculas. Found a large white Orchis in Oxey Wood of a curious species and very rare.
I watched a blue~cap or blue~titmouse feeding her young, whose nest was in a wall close to an orchard. She got cater~pillars out of the blossoms of the apple trees and leaves of the plum. She fetched 120 caterpillars in half an hour. Now suppose she only feeds them four times a day, a quart~er of an hour each time, she fetched no less than 480 caterpillars . . . . .

26th May 1825 Thursday.

Journal 1824-5

  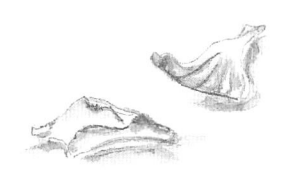 

~ On Snails ~.

The instinct of the snail is very remarkable and worthy of notice, tho such things are looked over with a careless eye — it has such a knowledge of it's own speed, that it can get home to a moment to be safe from the sun, as a moment too late would be it's death~ as soon as the sun has lost it's power to hurt, in the evening, it leaves it's hiding place in search of food which it is generally aware to find if it is a good way off~ it makes no stoppages in the road, but appears to be in great haste and when it has divided it's time to the utmost by travelling to such a length as will occupy all the rest of it's spare time to return, it's instinct will suddenly stop and feed on what it finds there and if it finds nothing it will go no further but return home~ wards and feed on what it chances to meet with, and after it gets home the sun shoud chance to be under a cloud, it will potter ab- out it's door~way to seek food, but it goes no further and is ready to hide when the sun looks out ~ when they find any food which suits them, they will feed on it till it lasts and travel to this same spot as accurately as if they knew geo~ graphy or was guided by a mariners compass ~ the power of instinct in the most trifling insect is very remarkable and displays the omnipotence of its maker in an illustrious man- ner, Nature is a fine preacher and her sermons are always wor th attention.

from *Natural History Letters 1825-37.*

~ The Red~bagged Bee~

The Red~bagged Bee, on never weary wings,
Pipes his small trumpet round the early flowers;
And white nettles by the hedge in Spring
Hears his low music all the sunny hours,
Till clouds come on and leaves the fally showers.
Herald of the Spring and music of wild blooms,
It seems the minstrel of Springs early flowers,
On banks, where the Red~nettle flower it comes
And there all the long sunny morning, hums.

28th May . Saturday
Found the old frog in my garden that has been there
this four years. I know it by a mark, which it received
from my spade four years ago. I thought it would die
of the wound, so I turned it up on a bed of flowers at the
end of the garden, which is thickly covered with ferns
and bluebells, I am glad to see it has recovered.

The Journal 1824 - 25

CLOCK - A - CLAY.

In the cowslip's peeps I lye,
Hidden from the buzzing fly,
While green grass beneath me lies,
Pearled with dew like fishes' eyes,
Here I lie, a clock-a-clay,
Waiting for the time of day.

While grassy forests quake surprise,
And wild winds sobs and sighs,
My gold home rocks as like to fall,
On it's pillars green and tall;
When pattering rain drives bye
A clock-a-clay keeps warm and dry.

Day by day and night by night,
All the week I hide from sight,
In the cowslip's peeps I lie,
In rain and dew still warm and dry,
Day and night and night and day,
Red and black-spotted clock-a-clay.

My home it shakes in wind and showers,
Pale green pillar top't wi' flowers,
Bending at the wild wind's breath,
Till I touch the grass beneath
Here still I live, lone clock-a-clay,
Waiting for the time of day.

82

~ Pale-green pillar top't wi flowers. ~

June

Now summer is in flower, and Nature's hum
Is never silent round her sultry bloom;
Insects, as small as dust, are never done
Wi' glittering dance, and reeling in the sun;
And green wood-fly, and blossom-haunting bee,
Are never weary of their melody.
Round field and hedge, now flowers in full glory twine,
Large bind-weed bells, wild hop, and streaked woodbine,
That lift athirst their slender-throated flowers,
Agape for dew-falls, and for honey showers;

These round each bush in sweet disorder run,
And spread their wild hues to the sultry sun.
Where its silk-netting lace, on twigs and leaves
The mottled spider, at eve's leisure, weaves
That every morning meet the poets eye,
      Like fairie's dew-wet dresses hung to dry...
            from Shepherd's Calendar June.

.....The wheat swells into ear, and hides below
The May-month wild flowers and their gaudy show,
Bright carlock, blue-cap and corn-poppy red,
Which in such clouds of colours widely spread,
That at the sun-rise, might to fancy's eye,
Seem to reflect the many coloured sky,
And leveret's seat, and lark, and partridge nest,
It leaves a schoolboy's height, in snugger rest,
And o'er the weeders labour overgrows;

Who now in merry groups, each morning goes.
To willow skirted meads wi' fork and rake,
The scented hay~cocks in long rows to make,
Where, their old visitors, in russet brown,
The hay~time butterflyes dance up and down;
And gad's, that teaze like wasps the timid maid
And drive the herd~boy's cows, to pond and shade....

From 'Shepherd's Calendar   'June'

......And now, when sheering of the flocks are done,
Some ancient customs, mix'd wi'harmless fun,
Crowns the swain's merry toils. The timid maid,
Pleased to be praised, and yet of praise affraid
Seeks her best flowers; not those of woods and fields,
But such as every farmer's garden yields ~

Fine cabbage~roses, painted like her face;
And shining pansy's trim'd in golden lace;

And tall tuft-larkheels, feather'd thick wi'flowers;
And woodbines, climbing o'er the door in bowers;.....

from Shepherd's Calendar June.

And London tufts of many a mottled hue

And pale-pink pea, and monkshead darkly blue

....And white and purple jilliflowers, that stay
Lingering, in blossom, summer half away;
And single blood-walls, of a luscious smell,
Old-fashion'd flowers which housewives love so well; ....

And columbines, stone~blue, or deep night-brown,
Their honey-comb-like blossoms hanging down,
Each cottage~garden's fond adopted child,
Tho' heaths still claim them, where they yet grow wild; ....
from Shepherd's Calendar June

.......Mong their old wild companions summer blooms;
Furze brake, and mozzling ling and golden broom;
Snapdragons, gaping, like to sleepy clowns,
And clipping pinks (which maidens Sunday gowns
Full often wear, catched at by toying chaps);
Pink as the ribbons around their snowy caps,
'Bess~in~her~bravery' too, of glowing dyes,
As deep as sunset's crimson pillow'd skyes,
And marjoram~notts, sweet~briar and ribbon~grass
And lavender, the choice of every lass,
And sprigs of Lad's~love all familiar names,
Which every garden thro' the village claims.....

From 'Shepherd's Calendar 'June'

3rd June. 1825.
Finished planting my auriculas: went a botanizing after ferns and orchises and caught a cold in the wet grass, which has made me as bad as ever. Got the tune of 'Highland Mary' from Wisdom Smith, a gipsy and pricked another sweet tune without a name as he fiddled it.

4th June. Saturday.
Saw three fellows at the end of Royce Wood, who, I found, were laying out the plan for an 'Iron Railway' from Manchester to London. It is to cross over Round~Oak Spring by Royce Wood corner for Woodcroft Castle, I little thought that fresh intrusions would interrupt and spoil my Solitudes;
After the Enclosure they will despoil a boggy place that is famous for orchises at Royce Wood end.

6th June. Monday.
Went to see Mrs. Bellar's garden at Wood~croft with Anna. Saw a scarlet anemone and white peony, both very handsome. The moat round the garden has a very fine effect, and the long bridges that cross it are made of planks and railed with crooked pieces of oak. I thought of the time of Cromwell while walking about it, and felt the difference. Swallows had several nests under the bridge.

10th June. Friday.
Saw the blue~grey or lead~coloured fly~catcher for the first time this season. They are called 'Egypt Birds' by the common people from their note, which seems to resemble the sound of the word 'Egypt', they build in old walls, like the redstart and grey wagtail.

14th June. Sunday.
Received a letter from Taylor in which he says that there is twice as much as he wants for the 'Shepherd's Calendar' and a few months back one of his causes for delay was that there was not enough to begin on. Nothing has made a wide difference here by time and left a puzzling paradox behind it, which tells he is a very dilatory chap. Received a parcel containing a present of a waistcoat and some fine polyanthus, Brompton stock, and geranium seed.

21st June. Tuesday.
Found a bird's nest in the thatch of a hovel gable~end in Billing's yard; think it is a fly catcher's. It resembles in colour and shape something of a chat or white throat, or more like the sedge bird than either. The female sits hard and the cock feeds her with caterpillars from the leaves of trees.

[extract from The Journal 1825]

~ papaver rhoeas ~

~ Common Poppy ~

The near-hand stubble field, with mellow glower
Showed the dimmed blaze of poppies still in flower.
John Clare

.....'Thus harvest ends it's busy reign,
And leaves the fields their peace again
Where Autumn's shadows idly muse......

July

The tottergrass upon the hill, from *Shepherd's Calendar*	102 – 103
Journal 12th ~ 29th July 1825	104 – 105
Flow on Winding River Poem	106 ~ 107
The Hollow Tree ~"~	108 ~
The Salter Tree —"~	108 ~
The Red Clover ~"~	~ 109
Old Pond Fenced all around Poem	110 ~
Summer ~"~	~ 111

August

Harvest approaches, from *Shepherd's Calendar*	112 ~ 113
~"~ ~"~ ~"~ ~"~ continued	114 ~ 115
The Ragwort Poem	116 ~
The Yarrow ~"~	~ 117
I Love at Early Morning Poem	118 ~
The Water Lilies —"~	~ 119
The Water Lily —"~	~ 119
The Skylark —"~	120 ~
Hares at Play ~"~	~ 121
Beans in Blossom —"~	122 ~
Summer Morning —"	~ 123
Journal. August 23rd 1825	~ 123

September

Harvest Awakes, from *Shepherd's Calendar*	124 ~ 125
Journal. Sept. 10th 1824	126 ~
Swift goes the Sooty Swallow. Poem	~ 127
Wild Bees ~"~	128 ~
The Dandelion —"~	~ 129
Prose on Poets	130 ~
The Bramble —"~	~ 131

July

Daughter of pastoral smells and sights,
And sultry days and dewy nights;

JULY, the month of Summer's prime,
Again resumes her busy time;
Scythes tinkle in each grassy dell,
Where solitude was want to dwell;
And meadows, they are mad with noise
Of laughing maids and shouting boys,
Making up the withering hay
With merry hearts as light as play.
The very insects on the ground
So nimbly bustle all around,
Among the grass, or dusty soil,
They seem partakers in the toil.
The landscape even reels with life,
While 'mid the busy stir and strife
Of industry, the shepherd still
Enjoys his summer dreams at will;
Bent o'er his book, or listless laid
Beneath the pasture's willow shade,
Whose foliage shines so cool and gray
Amid the sultry hues of day.......

....The breeze is stopt, the lazy bough
Hath not a leaf that dances now;
The tottergrass upon the hill,
And spiders threads are hanging still;
The feathers dropt from moorhens wing,
Which to the water's surface cling,
Are steadfast, and as heavy seem
As stones beneath them in the stream;
Hawkweed and groundsel's fairy downs
Unruffled keep their seeding crowns;
And in the oven~heated air
Not one light thing is floating there,
'Save that to the earnest eye,
The restless heat swims twittering bye......

from Shepherd's Calendar July

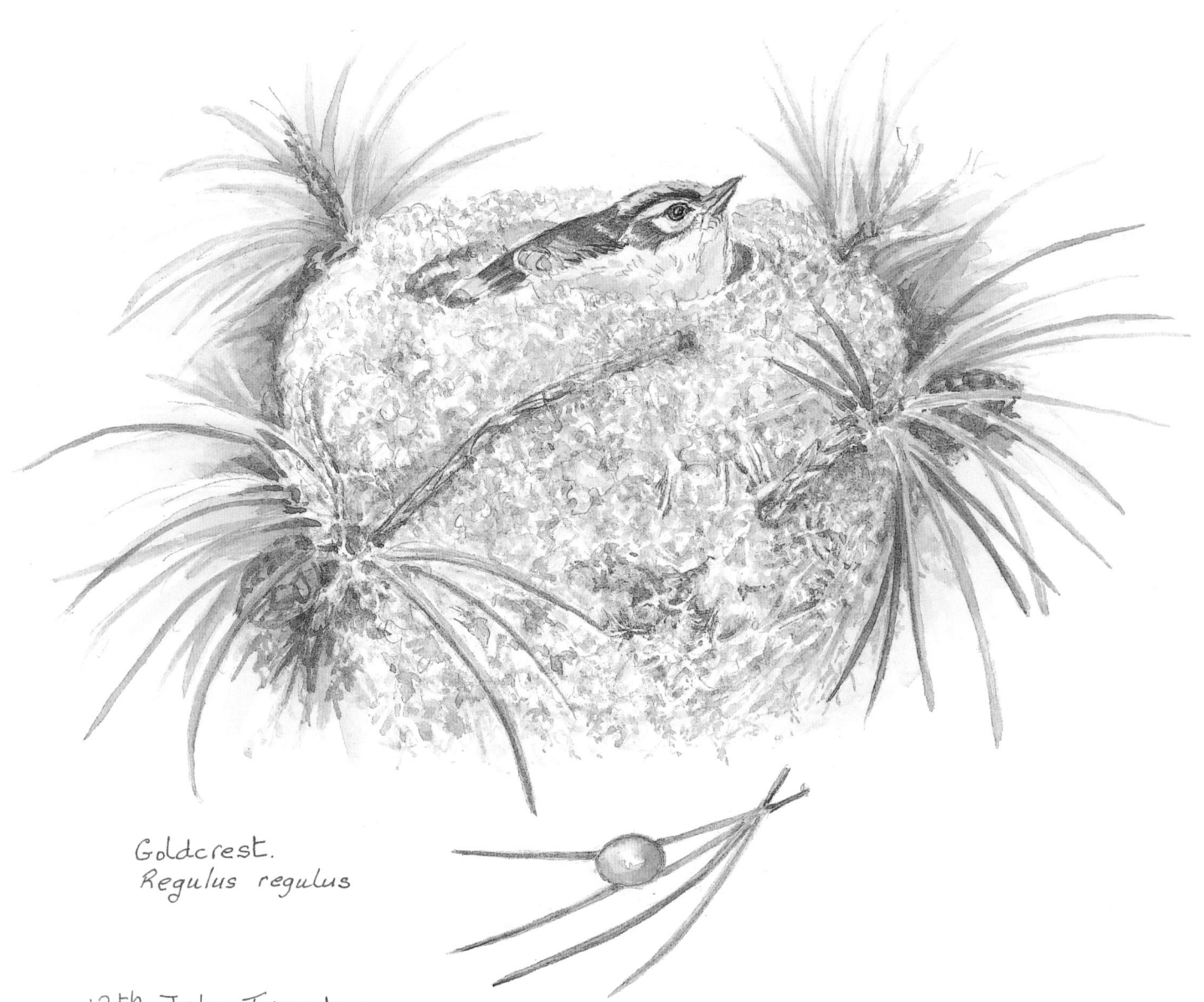

Goldcrest.
Regulus regulus

12th July. Tuesday.
Went today to see Artis : found him busy over his antiquities and fossils. He told me a curious thing about the manner in which the golden~crested wren builds her nest : he says it is the only English bird that suspends its nest, which hangs on three twigs of the fir~ branch, and it glues the eggs at the bottom of the nest, with the gum out of the tree, to keep them from being blown out by the wind, which often turns them upside-down without injury.

29th July. Friday.
Received a proof from Taylor. The plan is again altered, and he now intends to print the months only and leave out the tales; this plan is one that puts the worst first and leaves the best for a future opportunity. This proof contains 'February' and 'April'; The last is good for nothing and is not worth troubling the printers with. The Poem on Spring is the best in the bundle and would supply its place well.

MAGPIE.

builds on the highest branches of trees and in the thickest bushes,
Makes a covering over it's nest with two entrances, one facing the
West and the other the East, makes the outside of rough thorny
twigs and lines it with fibres of roots and twitch [grass] lays from
5 to 8 eggs of a watery green colour, thickly freckled with brown
spots, easily tamed and learned to talk.

  I kept one for years till it got drowned in a well, it used to see
itself in the water, I fancy it got down thinking to meet it, It used to
run away with the teaspoons or anything which it could come at and
would watch its opportunity as unceasingly as a reasoning being and
the moment it found it was not observed it would seize the thing it want-
ed and hasten out of the house to hide it in the garden where it would
let it lye a few days and then bring it in again — it imitated many
words readily and when it heard a sound or word that it could not im-
itate readily, it would become silent and pensive and sit ruminating
on an eldern tree and muttering as it were to itself some inaudible
words till at length it got by heart the thing it was aiming at and then
it was lively as ever and full of chatter as ever.

GREAT SPOTTED WOODPECKER.

this is smaller than the green one though it's habits are the same.
It is of a pied colour of brown and white with a red crown and a dingy
hue of red on the under parts of the belly — it taps more frequently
on the trees than the green one and makes the hole for its nest
in the grains. I know nothing of its eggs as I never have had, as yet,
the good fortune to meet with a nest — it seems to have a quick ear
at the approach of anything from which it seldom flyes, but nimbles
on the other side of the grain out of sight — there is a smaller one
of the same colour as this, but not so common. I have seen it often
but know nothing of it's habits any-way different from the former.
  from John Clare's List of Northamptonshire Birds.

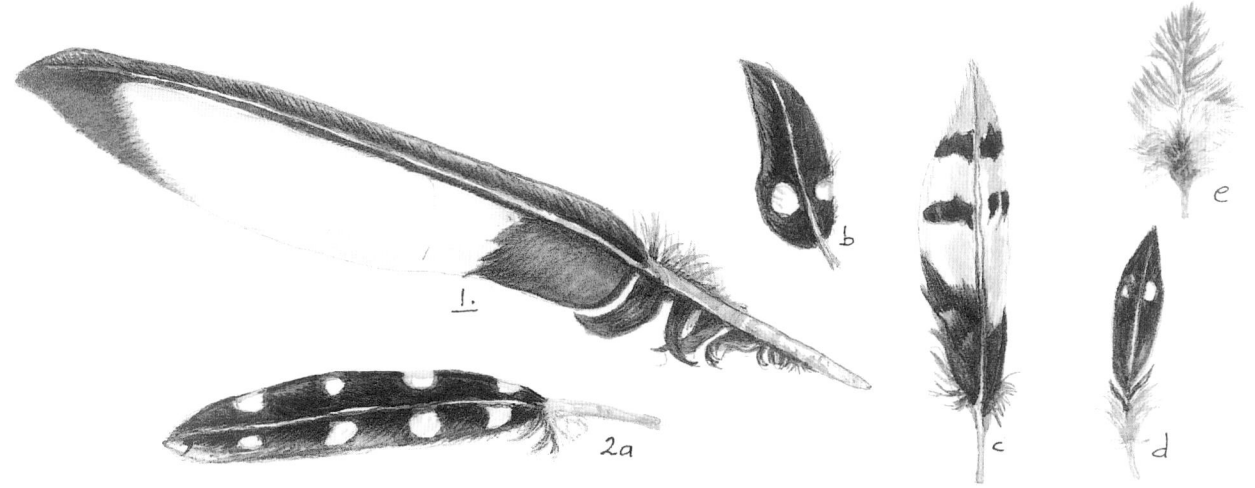

1. Magpie *Pica pica*   2. a – e Great spotted woodpecker. *Dendrocopos major.*

FLOW ON WINDING RIVER.

Flow on winding river, in silence for ever;
The sedge and flags rustle about in a bustle,
You are dear to my fancy, thou smooth flowing river,
The bullrush bows calm and there's peace in the hustle,
    As the boat gently glides,
    O'er thy soft flowing tides,
As the young maidens sail on, a sweet summer day.

The wavelets in ridges, by osiers, through bridges;
Neath the grey willows shade and nestling reeds made
Were dear to my fancy as onward they sail,
The osiers, they dip, in the rings lilys made
    And the maiden look'd red
    As the corn poppy bed
Or dog-rose that blushed in the shade.

The day was delightful, but gadflies were spiteful,
The hum of the bee, carolled merrily there,
The butterflies danced round the wild flowers delightful
And the old willows tossed their grey locks in the air,
    The boat softly rippled,
    Suspended oars drippled,
While the maidens were lovely and beautiously fair.

The boat gently pushes aside the bullrushes,
All gilt by the water and summer sunbeams
How soft the oar dashes the stream as it splashes
By the side of the boat wi its burden of dreams
    The rushing of waters
    The song o' earths daughters
How sweetly they sound in the 'plash of the streams.

1. Flowering rush. *Butomus umbellatus*. 2. Watermint *Mentha aquitica* 3. Bulrush *Typha latifolia*
4. Frogbit *Hydrocharis morsus-ranae* 5. Forget-me-not *Myosotis scorpioides*. 6. Marsh Mallow *Althaea officinalis*
7. Arrowhead *Sagittaria sagittifolia*

THE HOLLOW TREE.

How oft a summer shower hath started me
To seek for a shelter in a hollow tree,
Old huge ash dotterel wasted to a shell,
Whose vigorous head still grew and flourished well:
Where ten might sit upon the battered floor
And still look round discovering room for more:
And he who chose a hermit life to share
Might have a door and make a cabin there,
They seemed so like a house that our desires
Would call them so, and make our gipsy fires,
And eat field dinners of juicy peas,
Till we were wet and drabbled to the knees.
But in our old tree house rain as it might,
Not one drop fell, although it rained till night.

THE SALTER TREE.

Huge Elm thy rifted trunk all notched and scarred,
Like to a warriors destiny ~ I love
To stretch me often on such shadowed sward,
And hear the sighs of summer leaves above,
Or on thy buttressed roots to sit and lean
In careless attitude, and there reflect
On times, and deeds, and darings that have been.
Old cast aways, now swallowed in neglect
While thou art towering in thy strength of heart
Stirring the soul to vain imaginings,
In which lifes sordid being hath no part
The wind in that eternal ditty sings.
Humming of future things that burns the mind,
To leave some fragment of itself behind.

TO A RED CLOVER BLOSSOM.

Sweet bottled~shaped flower of lushy red,
  Born when the summer wakes her warmest breeze
Among the meadows waving grasses spread,
  Or neath the shade of hedge or clumping trees,
Bowing on slender stem thy heavy head
  In sweet delight I view thy summer bed
And hark the drone of heavy humble bees
  Along thy honeyed garden led
Down cornfield~striped baulks and pasture leas—
  Fond warmings of the soul that long has fled
Revives my bosum wi' their sweetness still,
  As I bend myself o'er thy ruddy pride
Recalling days I dropped upon a hill
  And cut my oaten trumpets by thy side.

109

The Old Pond Full of Flags.

The old pond full of flags and fenced around
With trees and bushes trailing to the ground
The water-reeds are all around the brink
And one clear place where cattle go to drink
From year to year the schoolboy thither steals
And muddys round the place to catch the eels
The cowboy often hiding from the flies
Lies there and plaits the rushcap as he lies
The hissing owl sits moping all the day
And hears his song and never flies away
The pinks nest hangs upon the branch so thin
The young ones caw and seem as tumbling in
While round them thrums the purple dragon flye
And great White-butterflye goes dancing bye

Summer.

How sweet when weary dropping on a bank
Turning a look around on things that be
Een feather-headed grasses spindling rank
A trembling to the breeze one loves to see
And yellow buttercups where many a bee
Comes buzzing to its head and bows it down
And the great dragonfly wi' gauzy wings
In gilded coat of purple-green or brown
That on broad leaves of hazel basking clings
Fond of the sunny day ~ and other things
Past counting pleases one while thus I lye
But still reflecting pains are not forgot
Summer, sometime, shall bless this spot when I
Hapt in the cold dark grave can heed it not.

111

August.

HARVEST approaches with its bustling day;
The wheat tans brown and barley bleaches grey;
In yellow garb the oatland intervenes,
And tawny glooms the valley thronged with beans...

....Amid the broils of harvest's weary reign,
How sweet the Sabbath wakes its rest again!
And on each weary mind what rapture dwells,
To hear once more its pleasant chiming bells,
That from each steeple, peeping here and there,
Murmer a soothing lullaby to care.
The shepherd, journeying on his morning rounds,
Pauses awhile to hear their pleasing sounds,
While the glad children, free from toil's employ,
Mimic the "ding dong" sounds and laugh for joy.
The fields themselves seem happy to be free,
Where insects chatter with unusual glee;
While Solitude, the grass and stubs among,
Appear to muse and listen to the song....

In calm delight, the Sabbath wears along;
Yet round the Cross, at noon, a tempted throng
Of little younkers, with their pence, repair
To buy the downy plum and luscious pear
That melts i' th' mouth, which gardeners never fail,
For gain's strong impulse, to expose for sale;
And on the circling Cross~steps in the sun,
Sit when the parson has his sermon done.
When gardeners that against his rules rebell,
Come wi' their baskets heaped with fruit to sell,
That thither all the season did pursue,
Wi' mellow gooseberry's of every hue,
Green ruffs, and raspberry reds, and drops of gold,
That makes mouths water often to behold! .....

from Shepherd's Calendar August.

113

....And currants red and white on cabbage leaves,
while childrens fingers itches to be thieves;
And black~red cherrys, shining to the sight,
As rich as brandy held before the light,
Now these are past, he still, as Sunday comes,
Sits on the cross wi' baskets heaped wi' plums,
And Jenitens streaked apples, sugar sweet,
Others, spice scented, ripening wi' the wheat....

.....And pears that melt 'inth' mouth like honey, which,
He oft declares, to make their spirits itch,
They are so juicy ripe, and better still
So rich! they e'en might suck them thro'a quill;
Here at their leisure gather many a clown,
To talk of grain and news about the town,
And here the boy wi' toils earned penny comes
In hurrying speed, to purchase pears or plums,
And o'er the basket hangs wi' many a smile,
Wi' hat in hand to hold his prize the while.....

from 'Shepherd's Calendar 'August'.

115

THE RAGWORT.

Ragwort thou humble flower with tattered leaves,
   I love to see thee come and litter gold;
What time the summer binds her russet sheaves
   Decking rude spots in beauties manifold,
   That without thee were dreary to behold,
Sunburnt and bare ~ the meadow bank, the baulk
   That leads a waggon way through mellow fields
   Rich with the tints that harvest's plenty yields
Browns of all hues ~ and everywhere I walk
   Thy waste of shining blossoms richly shields
The suntanned sward in splendid hues that burn
   So bright and glaring that the very light
Of the rich sunshine doth to paleness turn
   And seems but very shadows in thy sight.

THE YARROW.

Dweller in pastoral spots, life gladly learns
    That nature never mars her aim to please;
Thy dark leaves like to clumps of little ferns
    Imbues my walks with feelings such as these;
O'er topped with swarms of flowers that charms the night,
Some blushing into pink and others white,
    On meadow banks, roadsides and on the leas
Of rough neglected pastures ~ I delight
    More even than in gardens thus to stray
    Amid such scenes and mark thy hardy blooms,
    Peering into the Autumn's mellowing day;
The mower's scythe swept summer blooms away
    Where thou, defying dreariness, wilt come
Bidding the loneliest russet paths be gay.

EARLY MORNING.

I love at early morn, from new mown swath,
　　To see the startled frog his route pursue ;
To mark, while leaping o'er the dripping path,
　　His bright sides scatter dew,
The early lark that from its bustle flies,
　　To hail his matin new ;
　　　　And watch him to the skies.

To note on hedgerow baulks, in moisture spent,
　　The jetty snail creep from thorn,
With ernest heed and tremulous intent,
　　Frail brother of the morn,
That from the tiny bent's dew~misted leaves
　　Withdraws his timid horn,
　　　　And fearful visions weaves.

THE WATER LILIES.

The water lilies, white and yellow flowers,
    How beautiful they are upon the lake!
I've stood and looked upon the place for hours
    And thought how fine a garden they would make,
The pleasant leaves upon the water float;
    The dragon fly would come and stay for hours
And when the water pushed the pleasure boat
    Would find a safer place among the flowers:
They lay like beauty with a smiling face,
    And I have called them 'ladies of the Lake'!
I've brought the longest pole and stood for hours,
And tried for years, before I got those flowers!

The Water Lilies on the Meadow Stream

The water lilies on the meadow stream
    Again spread out their leaves of glossy green,
And some yet young in a rich copper gleam
    Scarce open in the sunny stream is seen,
Throwing a richness upon leisure's eye
    That thither wanders in a vacant joy;
While on the sloping banks luxuriant lie
    Tending of horse or cow the chubby boy,
Who in delighted whims will often throw
    Pebbles to hit and splash their sunny leaves,
Yet quickly dry again they shine and glow
    Like some rich vision that his eye deceives,
Spreading above the water day by day,
Safer than blooms among the meadow hay.

119

~ The Skylark ~

The rolls and harrows lie at rest beside
The battered road and, spreading far and wide
Above the russet clods, the corn is seen
Sprouting its spiry points of tender green,
Where squats the hare to terrors wide awake
Like some brown clod the harrows failed to break,
While neath the warm hedge boys stray far from home
To crop the early blossoms as they come;
Where buttercups will make them eager run
Opening their golden caskets to the sun
To who shall be first to pluck the prize;
And from their hurry, up the skylark flies
And o'er her half-formed nest with happy wings
Winnows the air ~ till in the clouds she sings.
Then hangs a dust spot in the sunny skies
And drops and drops till in her nest she lies
Where boys unheeding passed ~ ne'er dreaming then
That birds which flew so high ~ would drop again
To nests upon the ground where any thing
May come at to destroy. Had they the wing
Like such a bird, themselves would be too proud
And build on nothing but a passing cloud,
As free from danger as the heavens are free
From pain and toil ~ there would they build and be
And sail about the world to scenes unheard
of and unseen ~ O were they but a bird.
So think they while they listen to its song
And smile and fancy and so pass along
While its low nest moist with the dews of morn
Lie safely with the leveret in the corn.

~ Hares at Play ~

The birds have gone to bed, the cows are still
And sheep lie panting on each old mole-hill.
And underneath the willows grey-green bough
Like toil a resting ~ lies the fallow plough
The timid hares throw daylights fear away
On the lanes road to dust and dance and play
Then dabble in the grain by nought deterred
To lick the dewfall from the barleys beard
Then out they sturt again and round the hill
Like happy thoughts, dance, squat and loiter still
Till milking maidens in the early morn
Gingle their yokes and start them in the corn
Through well known beaten paths, each nimbling hare
Sturts quick as fear ~ and seeks it's hidden lair.

Beans in Blossom.

The southwest wind, how pleasant in the face
It breathes while, sauntering in a musing pace,
I roam these new-ploughed fields and by the side
Of this old wood, where happy abide
And the rich blackbird, through his golden bill
Utters wild music when the rest are still.
Now luscious comes the scent of blossomed beans
That o'er the path in rich disorder leans,
'Mid which the bees in busy songs and toils,
Load home luxuriantly their yellow spoils.
The herd-cows toss the molehills in their play
And often stand the stranger's steps at bay,
'Mid clover blossoms red and tawny white,
Strong scented with the summer's warm delight.

Summer Morning.

I love to peep out on a summers morn
Just as the scouting rabbit seeks her shed
And the coy hare squats nestling in the corn
Frit at the bow'd ear tottering o'er her head
And blundering pheasants that from covert spring
Their short sleep broke by early trampling feet
Making one startle wi' their rustling wings
As thro the boughs they seek more safe retreat
The little flower begem'd around wi' drops
That shine at sunrise like to burnished gold
So sweet to view the milk maid often stops
And wonders much such spangles to behold
The hedger too admires e'en deck the thorn
And thinks he sees no beauties like the morn.

Tuesday 23rd August 1825.

Found a most beautiful Death's-head moth caterpillar
in Billing's potatoes. It is about four and a half inches
long, of most beautiful rainbow colours.

September

..... The butterflye enjoys his hour,
And flirts, unchased, from flower to flower;
And humming bees, that morning calls
From out the low hut's mortar walls, ...

..... Loud are the morning's early sounds;
That farm and cottage yard surrounds,
The creaking noise of opening gate,
And clanking pumps, where boys await
With idle motion, to supply
The thirst of cattle crowding bye.
The low of cows and bark of dogs
And cackling hens and whining hogs
Swell high ~ while at the noise awoke
Old Goody seeks her milking cloak,
And hastens out to milk the cow,
And fills the troughs to feed the sow,
Or seeking old hens, laid astray,
Or from young chickens, drives away,
The circling kite that round them flyes,
Waiting the chance to seize the prize .....

Hogs trye thro' gates the street to gain,
And steal into the fields of grain;
From nights dull prison comes the duck
Waddling eager thro' the muck,
Squeezing thro' the orchard pales
Where mornings bounty rarely fails;
Eager gobbling as they pass
Dew worms thro' the padded grass,
Where blushing apples round and red,
Load down the boughs and pat the head
Of longing maid, that hither goes
To hang on lines, the drying cloaths;
Who views them oft with tempting eye
And steals one as she passes bye .....

from Shepherd's Calendar September

125

Swift Goes the Sooty Swallow

Swift goes the sooty swallow o'er the heath,
Swifter then skims the cloud rack of the skies,
As swiftly flies it's shadow underneath,
And on his wing the twittering sunbeam lies
As bright as water glitters in the eyes
Of those it passes ～ 'tis a pretty thing
The ornament of meadows ～and clear skies;
With dingy breast, and narrow pointed wing
It's daily twittering is a song to Spring.

Friday 10th September 1825.

My health would permit me do nothing more than take walks in
the garden today, What a sadly pleasing appearance gardens have
at this season!
    The tall gaudy hollyhock with its melacholy blooms stands bending
to the wind and bidding summer farewell, while the low asters, in
their pied lustre or red, white, and blue, bend beneath in pensive
silence, as though they mused over the days gone by and were sorrow-
ful. The swallows are flocking together in the skies, ready for de-
parture, and a crowd has dropt to rest on the walnut tree, where
they twitter as if they were telling their young stories of their long
journey, to cheer and check fear.

WILD BEES.

These children of the sun, which summer brings
As pastoral minstrels in her merry train,
Pipe rustic ballads upon busy wings
And glad the cotters quiet toils again:
The white~nosed bee, that bores its little hole
In mortared walls and pipes its symphonies,
And never absent couzin, black as coal,
That indian-like, bepaints its little thighs
With white and red, bedight for holiday,
Right early a morn do pipe and play
And with their legs, stroke slumber from their eyes
And aye so fond they of their singing seem
That in their holes abed at close of day
They still keep piping in their honey dreams.
And larger ones, that thrum on ruder pipe,
Round sweet smelling closen and rich woods,
Where tawny~white and red flushed clover buds
Shine bonnily and bean fields blossom ripe,
Shed dainty perfumes and give honey food
To these sweet poets of the sunny field.

Me, much delighting as I sawn along
The narrow path, that hay laid meadows yields,
Catching the windings of their wandering song.
The black and yellow bumble first on wing.
To buzz among the sallows early flowers
Hiding its nest in holes from fickle spring,
Who stints his rambles with her frequent showers,
And one that may for wiser piper pass
In livery dress half~sables and half red,
Who laps a moss~ball in the meadow grass
And hurds her stores when April showers have fled
And russet commoner, who knows the face
Of every blossom that the meadow brings,
Starting the traveller to a quicker pace,
By threatening round his head in many rings,
These sweeten summer in their happy glee
By giving for her, honey melodie.

1. Buff~tailed bumble~bee   2 carder~bee
3. White~tailed bumble~bee

The Dandelion.

This common dandelion ~ mark how fine
It's hue ~ the shadow of the Day's proud eye
Glows not more rich of gold; that nettle there,
Trod down by careless rustics every hour ~
Search but it's slightest blooms, king's cannot wear
Robe's prank't with half the splendour of a flower.

4. Mason bee   5. Davies colletes bee
6. Red~tailed bumble~bee   7. Mining~bee

On Favourite Poems and Poets

'For my part, I love to look on nature with a poetic feeling which magnifys the pleasure ~ I love to see the nightingale in its hazel retreat and the cuckoo hiding in its solitudes of oaken foliage and not examine their carcasses in glass cases, yet naturalists and botanists seem to have no taste for this practical feeling ~ they merely make collections of dryd specimens ~ classing them after Linnaeus into tribes and familys and there they delight to show them as a sort of ambitious fame, with them 'a bird in the hand is worth two in the bush' well everyone to his hobby'.

I have none of this curiosity about me 'tho I feel as happy as they can about finding a new species of field flower or butterflye which I have not seen before ~ yet I have no desire further to dry the plant or torture the butterflye by sticking it on a cork~board with a pin ~ I have no wish to do this if my feelings woud let me ~ I only crop the blossom of the flower or take the root from its solitudes if it woud grace my garden and wish the fluttering butterflye to settle till I can come up with it to examine the powderd colours on it's wings and then it may dance off again from fancyd dangers and welcome). I think your feelings are on the side of Poetry for I have no specimens to send you ~ so be as it may you must be content with my descriptions and observations ~ I always feel delighted when an object in nature brings up in ones mind an image of poetry that describes it from some favourite author ~ you have a better opportunity of consulting books than I have ~ therefore I will set down a list of favourite Poems and Poets who went to nature for their images so that you may consult them and share the feelings and pleasures which I describe ~ your favourite Chaucer is one ~ Passages in Spencer ~ Cowley's grasshopper and Swallow Passages in Shakespear ~ Milton's Allegro and Penseroso and Parts of Comus the Elizabethan Poets of glorious memory Grays Shepherds week Green's Spleen ~ Thomson's Seasons ~ Collin's Ode to Evening ~ Dyer's Grongar Hill and Fleece Shenstone's School mistress ~ Gray's Ode to Spring ~ T. Warton's April Summer Hamlet and Ode to a friend ~ Cowper's Task ~ Wordsworth Logans Ode to the Cuckoo ~ Langhorne's Fables of Flora ~ Jago's Blackbirds ~ Bloomfield Witchwood Forest Shooters hill etc with Hurdis's Evening walk in the village Curate and many others that may have slipped my memory'.

'the man of taste looks on the little Celandine in Spring and mutters in his mind some favourite lines from Wordsworths address to that flower he never sees the daisy without thinking of Burns and who sees the taller buttercup carpeting the closes in golden fringe without a remembrance of Chatterton's beautiful mention of it.'

From *Natural History Letters* 1825~37

The Bramble

Spontaneous flourisher in thickets lone
  Curving a most impenetrable way
To all save nutters when a tree has shown
  Ripe clusters to the autumn's mellow day ;
  And long the brustle of the rude affray
Clings to the branches ~ scraps of garments torn
    Of many hues : red, purple, green and grey,
From scrambling maid who ties the branches down
    And inly smiles at the strange garb she wears,
While rough in hasty speech the brushing clown
    Leg hoppled as in tethers turns and swears
And cuts the bramble strings with oath and frown,
    Yet scorn wronged bush, taste marks thee worthy praise,
    Green mid the underwood of winter days

Helleborus niger

~ Christmas Rose ~

I never want the Christmas Rose
To bloom before its time, ~
The Seasons each as God bestows
Are simple and sublime —.
John Clare.

..... The shepherd too, in great-coat wrapt,
And strawbands round his stockings lapt,
Wi' plodding dog that sheltering steals,
To shun the wind behind his heels,
Takes rough and smooth the Winter weather,
And paces thro' the snow together.....

October

Nature now spreads around, from *Shepherd's Calendar*   136~137
Journal Oct 20th 1824   138 ~
Evening Primrose.   Poem   ~ 139
Prose   Fen Description   Autumn   140 ~
Journal Oct 31st Sunday 1824   ~141
Autumn. Poem   142~143

November

The Village sleeps in Mist. from *Shepherd's Calendar*   144-145
Autumn Leaves   Poem   146 - 147
The Winters come   ~"~   148-149
Journal Nov 1st, 3rd, and 5th 1824   150-151
    ~"~   Nov 17th, 19th, and 20th 1824   152~
Written in November   Poem   ~153

December

Christmass is come. from *Shepherd's Calendar*   154~155
Beneath the branch of mizzletoe   156 - 157
Blackbirds and thrushes, *Nat. History Letters 1828*   158 ~
Journal Dec 16th ~ 29th 1824   ~159
The Winter's Spring.   Poem   160~161

Map of Helpston and Surrounding Countryside   162-163
Catalogue of Wild Field Flowers   164-171

October

.....The cotter journeying wi' his noisy swine,.
Along the wood-side where the brambles twine,
Shaking from dinted cups the acorns brown,
And from the hedges red haws dashing down;
The nutters, rustling in the yellow woods,
Scaring, from their snug lairs, the pheasants brood,
And squirrels secret toils oer winter dreams,
Picking the brown nuts from yellowing beams;
And hunters, from the thickets avenue
In scarlet jackets startling on the view,
Skimming a moment o'er the russet plain,
Then hiding in the coloured woods again.....

..... Oft dames, in faded cloak of red or grey,
Loitering along the morning's dripping way,
With wicker basket on their with'rd arms,
Searching the hedges of home close, or farms,
Where brashy elder trees, to autumn fade;
Each cotters mossy hut and garden shade,
Whose glossy berrys picturesquely weaves
Their swarthy bunches, mid the yellow leaves;
Where the pert sparrow stains his little bill,
And tutling robin picks his meal at will;
Black ripening to the wan suns misty ray.
Here the industrious huswifes wend their way,
Pulling the brittle branches carefully down,
And hawking loads of berrys to the town,
Wi unpretending skill, yet half devine,
To press and make their eldern~berry wine,
That bottled up, becomes a rousing charm,
To kindle winter's, icy bosom warm;
That wi' its merry partner, nut~brown beer,
Makes up the pedsant's Christmas~keeping cheer.....

from Shepherd's Calendar October

Wednesday 20ᵗʰ October.
Worked in the garden at making a shed for my auriculas.
The Michaelmas-daisy is in full flower, both the lilac-blue
and the white, thick set with its' little clustering stars of
flowers.
Thursday 21ˢᵗ October.
Took a walk in the fields. Gathered a bunch of wild flowers
that lingered in sheltered places as loath to die. The
ragwort lingers still in its yellow clusters, and the little heath-
bell or harvest-bell quakes to the wind under the quick
banks of warm furze. Clumps of wild marjoram are yet
in flower about the mole-hill banks, and clumps of Meadow-
sweet linger with a few bushes yet unfaded.

THE EVENING PRIMROSE

When once the sun sinks in the west,
And dewdrops pearl the evenings breast,
 Almost as pale as moonbeams are
 Or its companianble star,
The evening primrose opens anew
Its delicate blossoms to the dew,
 And shining hermit of the light,
 Wastes it's fair bloom upon the night,
Who, blindfold to its fond caresses,
Knows not the beauty it possesses,
 Thus it blooms on, till night is by
 And joy looks out with open eye,
'Bashed at the gaze it cannot shun
It faints and withers, and is done.

' The rawky mornings now are often frosty ~ and the grass and wild herbs
are often covered with rime as white as a shower of snow ~ in the fen greens-
ward closes, the pewit or lapwing may be seen in flocks of two or three hun-
dred together about Waldron Hall dabbling on the edges of the lakes, left
by the rains ~ it is pleasing to see the woods of oziers by the riverside
fading yellow. There are a few willow trees by the Hall or cottage ~ where
the crows sit in the old nests as if it were spring though perhaps they may
do it to get from the cold, for there is a little crizzling ice on the edges of
the water in some places such as ruts and horsefootings ~ Now the man is put-
ting off his boat to ferry over the water, where an odd passenger may now
and then, call to be ferried over the lake to the other bank or high road ~
   The ozier hedges and holts are withered; yellow and white~thorn hedges
are getting thin of leaves and so crowded with aws, that bye & bye the fields
will be dressed in nothing but crimson and scarlet ~ nature like simplicity is
beautifull in every dress she chuses to put on with the seasons ~ even win-
ter with his doublet of snows and hoar frost can make himself agreeable
when he chuses to give people leave to go out of doors ~ I love to clamber
over these bridge~walls and when I get off the banks on the road, I instinc-
lively look both ways to see if any passengers are going or coming, or carts,
or waggons passing. Now here is a stile, partitioning off somebody's part-
ition of the bank, but the middle rail is off, so I stoop under to get through
instead of climbing over it ~ there is a pair of harrows painted red, standing
on end against the thorn hedge ~ in another ground an old plough stands
on it's beam ends against a dotterel tree, sometimes we see a roller lying
in one corner and broken trays and an old gate off the hooks waiting to be
repaired till repairs are useless ~ even these rustic implements and
appendages of husbandry blend with nature and look pleasing in the
fields.

Extract from 'Fen Description' 1841

31st October. Tuesday. 1824
Took a walk, got some branches of the spindle tree, with it's pink-coloured
berries that shine beautifully in the pale sun. Found for the first time,"the
herb~true~love' or 'One Berry in Oxey Wood.
Brought a root home to set in my garden.

AUTUMN.

The autumn day it fades away,
The fields are wet and dreary;
The rude storm takes the flowers of May,
And nature seemeth weary.
The partridge coveys shunning fate,
Hide in the bleaching stubble;
And many a bird without its mate,
Mourns o'er its lonely trouble.

Black Bryony

Tamus communis

On 'awthorns shine the crimson awe,
Where spring brought may-day blossoms;
Decay is nature's cheerless law,
Life's winter in our bosoms.
The fields are brown and naked all,
But hedges still are green;
But storms shall come at autumns fall,
And not a leaf be seen!

Yet happy love that warms the heart,
Through darkest storms severe;
Keeps many a tender flower to start,—
When Spring shall re-appear,
Affections hope shall roseys meet;
Like those of summer bloom:—
And joys, and flowers, smell as sweet,
In seasons yet to come.

Hawthorn
Crataegus oxyacantha

NOVEMBER

The village sleeps in mist from morn 'til noon;
And, if the sun wades thro', tis with a face,
Beamless and pale and round, as if the moon,
When done the journey of it's nightly race,
Had found him sleeping and supplyd his place.
For days the shepherds in the fields may be,
Nor mark a patch of sky ~ blindfold they trace,
The plains, that seem wi' out a bush or tree,
Whistling aloud, by guess, to flocks they cannot see.

.... The Owlet leaves her hiding~place at noon,
And flaps her grey wings in the doubting light;
The hoarse jay screams to see her out so soon,
And small birds chirp and startle with affright;
Much doth it scare, – the superstitious white,
Who dreams of sorry luck, and sore dismay;
While cow~boys think the day a dream of night,
And oft grow fearful on their lonely way,
Who fancy ghosts may wake, and leave their graves by day.

..... Thus wears the month along, in checker'd moods,
Sunshine and shadows, tempests loud, and calms;
One hour dies silent o'er the sleepy woods,
The next wakes loud with unexpected storms;
A dreary nakedness the fields deforms —
Yet many a rural sound and rural sight,
Live in the village still about the farms,
Where toil's rude uproar hums from morn till night
Noises, in which the ear of industry delights.

At length the noise of busy toil is still,
And industry awhile her care foregoes;
When Winter comes in earnest to fulfil
Her yearly task, at bleak November's close,
And stops the plough, and hides the field in snows;
When frost locks up the stream in chill delay,
And mellows on the hedge the purple sloes
For little birds — Then Toil hath time for play,
And nought but thresher's flails awake the dreary day.

from Shepherd's Calendar. November

I love the fitfull gusts, that shakes
    The casement all the day,
And from the mossy elm tree takes
    The faded leaf away,
Twirling it by the window pane,
With thousands of others down the lane.

I love to see the shaking twig
    Dance till the shut of eve,
The sparrow on the cottage rig,
    Whose chirp would make believe,
That spring was just now flirting by
I' summers lap with flowers to lie.

I love to see the cottage smoke,
    Curl upward through the naked trees;
The pigeons nestled round the cote
    On dull november days like these,
The cock upon the dunghill crowing,
The mill sails on the heath agoing.

Monday 1st November 1825.
Took a walk to Lolham Bridge to hunt for a species of fern
That used to grow on some willow tree heads in Lolham Lane
when I was a boy, but could find none. Got some of the yellow
water~lily from the pits, which the floods had washed up, to
set in an old water~tub in the garden, and to try some on land
in a swaily corner, where horse~blob thrives, which is a water~
flower.
Listened in the evening to Glinton bells at the top of the
garden. I always feel melancholy at this season to hear
them; and yet it is a pleasure.

                              I'm pleased at yet I'm sad.

3rd November 1824. WEDNESDAY.

Took a walk with John Billings to Swordy Well, to gather some 'old~
man's beard', which hangs about the hedges in full bloom. It's downy
clusters of artifical~like flowers appear at first as if the hedges
was littered with bunches of white cotton. Went into Hilly wood and
found a beautiful species of fern on a sallow stoven in a pit, which
I have not seen before. There are five sorts growing about the woods
here; the common~brake, the fox~fern, the hart's tongue and the
polypody, two sorts the tall and the dwarf.

6ᵀᴴ November, Saturday.   Took a walk in the fields. The oaks are beg~
inning to turn reddish~brown and the winds have stripped some nearly
bare. The underwood's last leaves are in their gayest yellows. This Aut~
umn seems to put on bridal colours for a shroud. The little harvest~bell
is still in bloom, trembling to the cold wind, almost the only flower living
save the 'old man's beard', or Travellers Joy, on the hedge.

15ᵀᴴ November. Monday. Went to gather pooties on the Roman bank for
a collection. Found a scarce sort of which I only saw two in my life,
one picked up under a hedge at Peakirk town end and another in
Bainton Meadow. It's colour is a fine sunny~yellow, larger than the com~
mon sort and round the rim of the base is a black edging which ex~
tends no further than the rim. It is not in the collection at the British
Museum.

The Journal 1824-25.

17th Nov. Wednesday.

The crysanthemums are in full flower. What a beautiful heart~
cheering to the different seasons nature has provided in her
continual successions of bloom of flowers!....the little aconite
peeps its yellow flowers, then the snowdrops, and further on the
crocus dropping in before the summer multitude; and after their
departure the tall hollyhock and the little aster bloom in their showy
colours; then comes the Michaelmas daisy, and lastly the crysanthe~
mums; while the China roses

all the year
Or in the bud or in the bloom appear.

19th November, friday.

Had a visit from my old friend Henderson, and I felt revived as I was very dull before. He had pleasing news to deliver me, having discovered a new species of fern a few days back, growing among the bogs on Whittlesey Mere: and our talk was of ferns for the day.

He tells me there are twenty~four different species, or more, natives of England and Scotland. One of the finest of the latter is called the Maidenhair, growing in rock~clefts.

20th November, Saturday.

Went out to hunt the Hart's~tongue species of ferns and fell in with the ruins of the old castle in Ashton Lawn; but found none. It's commonest place is in the wells, in the crevices of the walls, but I have found it growing about the badger~holes in Open Copy Wood. Got very wet and returned home. Finished the eighth chapter of my life.

Written in November.

Autumn, I love thy latter end to view
In cold Novembers day so bleak and bare
When like life's dwindl'd thread worn nearly thro
Wi lingering pottering pace and head bleached bare
Thou like an old man bids the world adieu
I love thee well, and often when a child
Have roamed the bare brown heath a flower to find
And in the moss~clad vale and wood bank wild
Have cropt the little bell flowers paley blue
That trembling peept the sheltering bush behind
When winnowing north winds cold and blealy blew
How have I joy'd wi dithering hands to find
Each fading flower and still how sweet the blast
Wou'd bleak November hour restore the joy that's past.

DECEMBER.

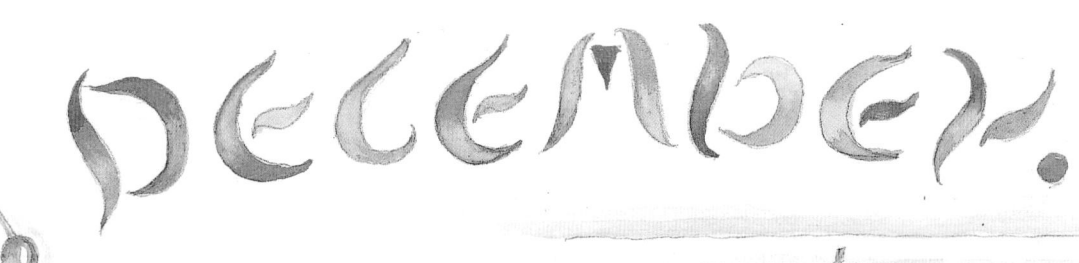

Christmass is come, and every hearth
   Makes room to give him welcome now,
E'en want will dry its tears in mirth,
   And crown him with a holly bough;
Tho' tramping 'neath a winter sky,
   O'er snow track paths and ryhmey stiles,
The hus~wife sets her spinning bye
   And bids him welcome wi' her smiles.

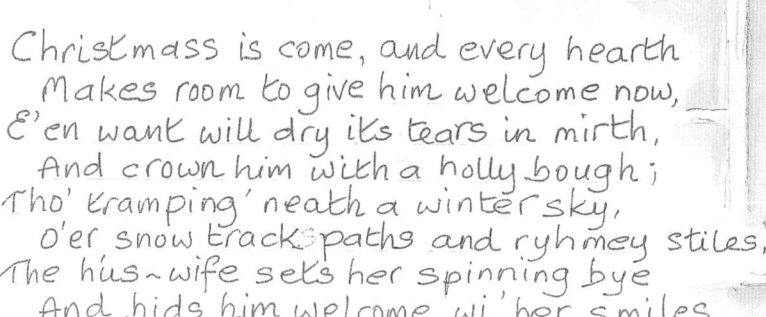

Each house is swept the day before,
   And windows stuck with ever~greens,
The snow is besom'd from the door,
   And comfort crowns the cottage scenes.
Gilt holly, with it's thorny pricks
   And yew and box, with berries small,
These deck the unused candle sticks,
   And pictures hanging by the wall.

Neighbours resume their annual cheer,
   Wishing, wi' smiles and spirits high,
Glad Christmass and a Happy Year,'
   To every morning passer~bye i
Milkmaids their Christmass journeys go,
   Accompany'd with favour'd swain i
And childern pace the crumping snow,
   To taste their granny's cake again.....

from 'Shepherd's Calendar. December

Hung wi' the ivys veining bough,
   The ash trees round the cottage farm,
Are often stript of branches now,
   The cotters Christmass hearth to warm;
He swings and twists his hazel band,
   And lops them off with sharpened hook,
And oft brings ivy in his hand,
   To decorate the chimney nook.....

.....The shepherd, now no more afraid,
   Since custom doth the chance bestow,
Starts up to kiss the giggling maid,
   Beneath the branch of mizzletoe
That 'neath each cottage beam is seen,
   With pearl~like~berrys shining gay;
The shadow still of what hath been,
   Which fashion yearly fades away.

And singers too, a merry throng,
   At early morn, with simple skill,
Yet imitate the angels song,
   And chant their Christmass ditty still;
And 'mid the storm that dies and swells
   By fits – in hummings softly steals
The music of the village bells,
   Ringing round their merry peals....

.... And oft for pence and spicy ale,
   With winter nosegays pinn'd before,
The wassail~singer tells her tale,
   And drawls her Christmass carols o'er
While 'prentise boy, with ruddy face,
   And rhyme~bepowder'd dancy locks
From door to door with happy pace,
   Runs round to claim his "christmass box."

Blackbirds and Thrushes particularly the former, feed in winters upon the shell snail-horns by hunting them from the hedge bottoms and wood-stulps, and taking them to a stone, where they break them in a very dexterous manner. Any curious observer of nature, may see in hard frosts, the shells of pootys thickly littered round a stone in the lanes and if he waits a short time, he will quickly see one of these birds coming with a snail horn in his bill, which he constantly taps on a stone till it is broken, he then extracts the snail and like a true sportsman eagerly hastens to hunt them again in the hedges or woods, where a frequent rustle of their little feet is heard among the dead leaves.

From 'Natural History Letters 1825-37

16th December. Thursday 1825.
Saw Henderson's collection of ferns, which is far from complete,
though some of them are beautiful. Learned from him of a sin-
gular instinct in plants of the creeping kind, some having a
propensity to twine to the left in their climbing, and others to
the right: the woodbine seems to twine to the left and the trav-
eller's joy to the right; but this is not an invariable fact.

Christmas Day, Saturday.
Gathered a handful of daisies in full bloom; saw a woodbine
and dog rose in the woods putting out in full leaf, and a primrose
root full of ripe flowers. What a day this used to be when (I was)
a boy! How eager I used to attend the church to see it stuck
with evergreens (emblems of eternity), and the cottage windows
and the picture ballads on the wall all stuck with ivy, holly, box
and yew! Such feelings are past and 'all this world is proud of.'

29th Dec. Wednesday.
Went with neighbour Billings to Southey Wood and Gees Holt to
hunt ferns: found none. Met with a new species of Moss fern,
striped, growing on a common species like the mistle~toe on a
thorn. It is a sort of moss mistletoe. Preserved a specimen.
Saw a branch of blackthorn, dog~rose, and eldern, in full leafall
in one hedgerow. Saw a bumbarrel with moss as if building a nest.

The Journal 1824 - 25.

THE WINTERS SPRING

The winter comes, I walk alone,
    I want no birds to sing,
To those who keep their hearts their own
    The Winter is the Spring.
No flowers to please ~ no bees to hum,
    The coming Springs already come.

I never want the Christmass rose
    To come before its time,
The seasons each as God bestows
    Are simple and sublime,
I love to see the snow~storm hing,
    'Tis but the Winter garb of Spring.

I never want the grass to bloom,
    The snow-storms best in white.
I love to see the tempest come,
    And love its piercing light.
The dazzled eyes that love to cling,
    O'er snow-white meadows, see the Spring.

I love the snow the crimpling snow
    That hangs on everything,
It covers everything below
    Like white-doves brooding wing;
A landscape to the aching sight,
    A vast expanse of dazzling light.

It is the foliage of the woods
    That winters bring, the dress,
White easter of the year in bud,
    That makes the winters Spring,
The frost and snow his posys bring,
    Nature's white spirits of the Spring

161

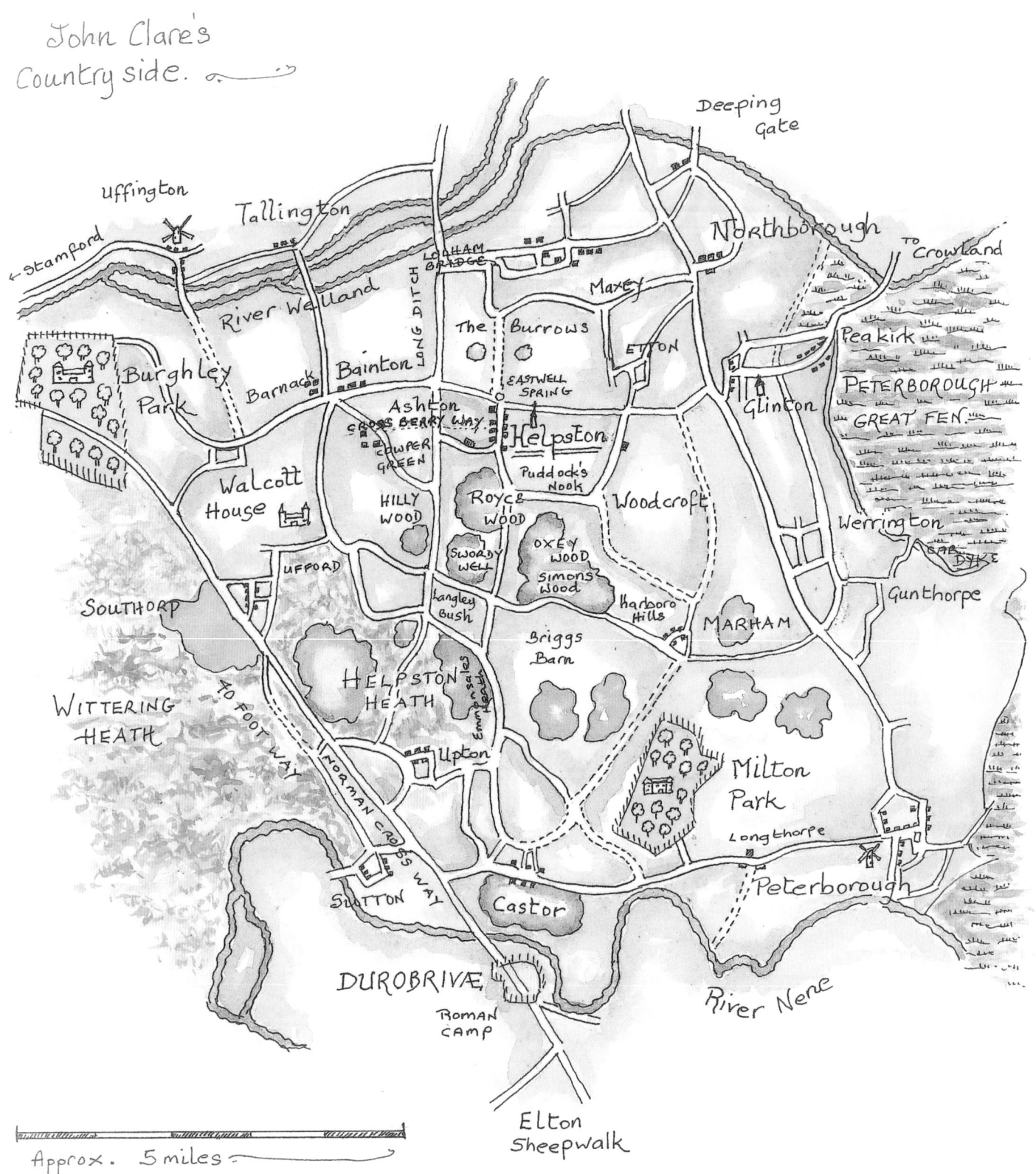

John Clare's
Countryside.

Map labels (clockwise / by region):

Deeping Gate · Uffington · Tallington · Northborough · To Crowland · ←Stamford · River Welland · Long Ditch · Lolham Bridge · Maxey · Etton · Pea kirk · PETERBOROUGH GREAT FEN · The Burrows · Glinton · Burghley Park · Barnack · Bainton · Ashton · Eastwell Spring · Cross Berry Way · Helpston · Cowper Green · Puddock's Nook · Woodcroft · Werrington · Car Dyke · Walcott House · Hilly Wood · Royce Wood · Oxey Wood · Simons Wood · Gunthorpe · Ufford · Swordy Well · Langley Bush · Harboro Hills · MARHAM · Southorp · Briggs Barn · Emmonsales Heath · Milton Park · WITTERING HEATH · HELPSTON HEATH · 40 Foot Way · Norman Cross Way · Upton · Longthorpe · Peterborough · Sutton · Castor · River Nene · DUROBRIVÆ · Roman Camp · Elton Sheepwalk

Approx. 5 miles

John Clare's writings included the names of many places he grew to love and know so well in the countryside around his birthplace and home, the village of Helpston in Northamptonshire, England.

Here he found and described 135 wildflowers in his poetry, some recorded for the first time in his home county. (Listed in the following pages 164 – 171).

Over 200 species of birds appear in his *Journal 1824-5*, his *Natural History Letters 1825 – 37* and in his *List of Northamptonshire Birds*.

He married Martha Turner (Patty) in 1820. They had 9 children, 7 surviving to adulthood. He died in 1864 and is buried at Helpston.

Dear heart and can it be that such raptures meet decay, I thought them all eternal when by Langley Bush I lay~

~ Went out to hunt the Hart's-tongue species of fern and fell in with the ruins of old Castle in Ashton Lawn.

~ went to gather poolies on the Roman Bank for a collection][When I used to lie and sing by old Castle fells bowing spring~

~Helpston~

Clinton thy taper spire predominates over the level landscape and the mind musing][When

on Casterton cowpasture on a Summer's night~

When jumping time away on old Crossberry way, and

they lost the May~

walk today and heard the Nightingale for the first time this season in Royce wood, just at the town end~

eating haws like sugar plums

~I went to take my

~Whittlesea Mere~

the daisy gemmed in dew][Weds. 4th March, The birds were singing in Oxey Wood at Six o'clock this evening as loud and various as in May.~

~Rotten Moor~ Open Copy

~Barnton Meadow

~Pea kirk~

~ The Gloworm is a sort of catterpillar insect and thousands of them may be seen on Sneap Green, Puddocks Nook, and Hilly Snow, where bramble bushes grew and

~ When I think of old

~Simons Wood for a sucker of the Barberry bush to set in my garden

~east~ Well moor~ Bush close~

~went to

HELPSTON 10 MILES

I

......." My wild field catalogue of flowers,
   Grows in my rhymes as thick as showers,
   Tedious and long as they may be,
   To some ; they never weary me.
   Then wood and mead and field of grain
   I could hunt o'er and o'er again
   And talk to every blossom wild
   Fond as a parent to a child......."___

                    from 'Shepherd's Calendar' May.

A nemone *	Anemone nemorosa	
(Wood or Windflower)		
ngelica, Wild *	Angelica sylvestris	
Ash, Common	Fraxinus excelsior	

~

B asil, Wild 2.	Acinos arvensis.
eech	Fagus sylvatica
Bell Flower	Campanula trachelium
Bent, Common *	Agrostis capillaris
Betony, Purple *	Stachys officinalis
Bindweed, Field	Convolvulus arvensis
Bindweed, Hedge *	Calystegia sepium
Birch, Common	Betula alba
Birdsfoot Trefoil 3.	Lotus corniculatus
Blackthorn, Sloe	Prunis spinosa
Bluebell	Endymion non-scriptus
Box	Buxus sempervirens
Bramble, Blackberry	Rubus fruticosus
Bryony, Black	Tamus communis
Bryony, White	Bryonia cretica
Brake, Bracken fern.	Pteridium aquilinium
Bugle, Common or Blue *	Ajuga reptens
Bugloss, Vipers	Echium vulgare

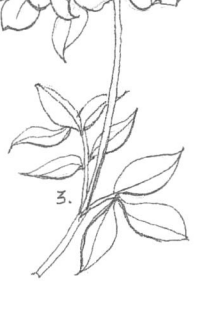

* first record in Northamptonshire.

.........Bulrush *   Scirpus lacustris
Burdock *   Arctium minus
Bur~Reed, Branched *   Sparganium erectum
Butterbur   Petasites hybridus
Buttercup, Bulbous   Ranunculus bulbosus
   (Kingcup)   ~
Buttercup, Meadow 4.   { R. acris
   (Yellowcup, Crowflower)   {   ~

Celandine, Lesser   { R. ficaria
   (Pilewort)   {   ~
Charlock   Sinapis arvensis
Cherry, Wild   Prunus avium
Chickweed, Common   Stellaria media
Cinquefoil, Creeping *   Potentilla reptans
Clover, Red 5.   Trifolium pratense
Clover, White   T. repens
Columbine   Aquilegia vulgaris
Cornflower (Blue~cap)   Centaurea cyanus
Cow Parsley   Anthriscus sylvestris
Cowslip   Primula veris
Couch Grass   { Elytrigia repens
      (twitchgrass)   {   ~
Crab Apple   Malus sylvestris

Daffodil, Wild   Narcissus pseudonarcissus
Daisy 6.   Bellis perennis
Dandelion   Taxaxacum vulgaria
Dewberry   Rubus caesius
Dog's Mercury   Mercurialis perennis

Elder, Common   Sambucus nigra
Elm,   Common   Ullmus procera

Forget-me-not, Field   *Myosotis arvensis*
Forget-me-not, Water * 7.   *M. scorpioides*
Foxglove   *Digitalis purpurea*
Fumitory, Common   *Fumaria officinalis*

~

Germander Speedwell 10.   *Veronica chamaedrys*
Gorse, Common Furze   *Ulex europaeus*
Groundsel   *Senecio vulgaris*

~

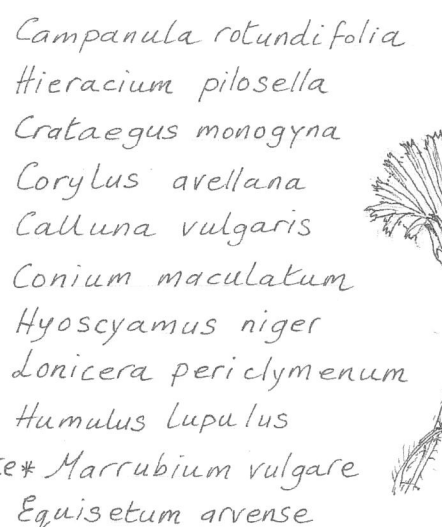

Harebell 8.   *Campanula rotundifolia*
Hawkweed, Mouse-ear 11.   *Hieracium pilosella*
Hawthorn or May-Tree   *Crataegus monogyna*
Hazel, Common   *Corylus avellana*
Heather, Ling   *Calluna vulgaris*
Hemlock *   *Conium maculatum*
Henbane   *Hyoscyamus niger*
Honeysuckle, Common *   *Lonicera periclymenum*
Hop, Wild *   *Humulus lupulus*
Horehound, Common or White *   *Marrubium vulgare*
Horsetail *   *Equisetum arvense*
House Leek *   *Sempervivium tectorum*

~

Iris, Yellow Flag *   *Iris pseudacorus*
Ivy *   *Hedera helix*

~

Knapweed, Common   *Centurea nigra*

~

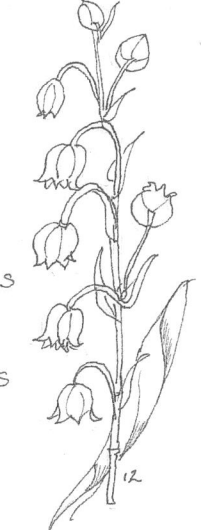

Ladies Smock *   *Cardamine pratensis*
  (Cuckoo-flower) 9.

~

Lily-of-the-Valley 12.   *Convallaria majalis*
Lime, Common *   *Tilia x vulgaris*
Lord's-and-Ladies   { *Arum maculatum.*
  (cuckoo-Pint)

~

Mallow, Common	Malva sylvestris
Maple, Field	Acer campestre
Marigold, Marsh *	Caltha palustris
Marjoram, Wild	Origanum vulgare
Meadow-Sweet	Spiraea ulmaria
Mint, Water *	Mentha aquatica
Mistle toe	Viscum album
Mullein, Great *	Verbascum thapsus

13.

Nettle, Red [14]	Lamium purpureum
Nettle, Stinging *	Urtica dioica
Nettle, White	Lamium album

Oak	Quercus robur
Orchid, Bee	Orchis apifera
~~ , Early, Purple [15] *	O. mascula
~~ , Spider, Early	O. ophrys sphegodes
~~ , Heath, Spotted	O. maculata

14

15.

"Haunting the mossy steps to botanize
    And hunt the Orchis tribes where nature's skill
Doth like my thoughts run into phantasies,
    Spider and Bee all mimicking at will,
Displaying powers that fool the proudly wise,
    Showing the wonders of great nature's plan
In trifles insignificant and small.
    Puzzling the power of that great trifle man.
Who finds no reason to be proud at all." ——
                M.S. Poems - 'Swardy Well'.

~

| Osier * | Salix viminalis |
| Oxeye Daisy | Leucanthemum vulgare |

Pellitory-of-the-wall	Parietaria judaica
Pine, Scots	Pinus sylvestris
Plantain	Plantago major
Ploughman's-Spikenard	Inula conyzae
Plum, Wild *	Prunus domestica
Poplar, Grey *	Populus × canescens
Poppy, Corn	Papaver rhoeas
Primrose 16	Primula vulgaris
Privet, Wild *	Ligustrum vulgare
Purple-loosestrife *	Lythrum salicarea

~

Quaking Grass * 17.	Briza media
(totty-grass)	

~

Ragged-Robin 18.	Lychnis flos-cuculi
Ragwort, Common	Phragmites australis
Rest Harrow	Ononis repens
Rose, Dog	Rosa canina
Rose, Sweet Briar	R. rubiginosa
Rush, Compact *	Juncus conglomeratus
Rush, Hard	J. inflexus
Rush, Wood, small-reed	Calamagrostis epigejos

Salad burnet	Sanguisorba minor
Scarlet pimpernel 19.	Anagallis arvensis
Sedge, Greater Pond *	Carex riparia
Shepherd's-Purse *	Capsella bursa-pastoris
Silverweed	Potentilla anserina
Spurge, Laurel	Daphne laureola
Strawberry, Wild * 20	Fragaria vesca
Sycamore	Acer pseudoplatanus

Teasel, Wild	Dipsacus fullonum
Thistle, Creeping [21]	Cirsium arvense
— , Marsh Sow-	Cirsium palustre
— , Smooth Sow-	Sonchus oleraceus
— , Spear [Bull]	Cirsium lanceolatum
Thyme, Breckland	Thymus serpyllum
Timothy Grass *	Phleum pratense
Traveller's-joy	Clematis vitalba
Tussock Grass	Deschampsia cespitosa

~

Violet, Sweet 22	Viola odorata

~

Watercress 23	Rorippa nasturtium aquaticum
Water-Lily White	Nymphaea alba
Water-Lily, Yellow	Nuphar lutea
[Brandy Balls]	
Water Meadow Grass *	Glyceria maxima
Weld	Reseda luteola
Willow, Goat 24 *	Salix caprea
Willow, White *	S. alba

" Pendant o'er rude old ponds, or leaning o'er
    The woodland's mossy rails, the Sallows now
Put on their golden liveries, and restore
    The Spring to splendid memories, ere a bough
Of whitethorn shows a leaf to say 'it's come :
    And through the leafless underwood rich stains
Of sunny gold show where the Sallows bloom,
    Like sunshine in dark places, and gold veins
Mapping the russet landscape into smiles
    At Spring's approach : nor hath the Sallow palms
A peer for richness : ploughmen in their toils
    Will crop a branch, 'smit with its golden charms"— m.s. Poems

~

Woody Nightshade or Bittersweet.   Solanum dulcamara

~

GLOSSARY

		Page			Page
awes	fruit of the hawthorn	140	hing	to hang	38
baulk	strip of grass between ploughed land	109	jeniten	variety of apple	114
bents	coarse grass, stalks etc	37	jilliflowers	flowers that grow in July, (wallflowers etc)	26 + 92
bess-in-her bravery	double-petalled daisy	94	King cup	marsh marigold	52
bloodwalls	dark double wallflower	92	larkheels	larkspur	89
blue cap	1, cornflower, 2, blue-tit	79	lad's love	southern wood	94
brakes	ferns	94	London tufts	sweet williams	90
brustle	bustle, rustle around	131	mozzling	mottled, various colours	94
bumbarrel	long-tailed tit	159	nimbles	move quickly	105
carlock	charlock, wild mustard	86	peep	single flower in a cluster	82
clipping pinks	small carnation	94	pettichap	chiffchaff	48
clock-a-clay	ladybird	82	pink	chaffinch	36
closen	small enclosure	128	pooty	snail	42
clown	rustic, worker	115	prank	adorn or decorate	129
cotter	cottage dweller	128	redcap	goldfinch	49
crowflower	buttercup	174	rawky	misty, foggy	140
dinted	dented or dimpled	137	sawn	saunter, loiter	128
dotterel	old pollarded tree	43	starnels	starlings	23
drabbled	draggled and muddied	108	stoven	stump	150
eldern	elderberry	30	strunt	strutting, cocky	30
fluskering	fluttering its wings	43	stulps	stump of a tree	44
foddering boy	boy who feeds hay to cattle	29	sturt	startle, dash away	121
foulroyce	dogwood	32	swaily	shady, cool	149
fret	thaw	30	swathy	swarthy	23
furze linnet	furze or goss lark	49	tippet	billet	35
gadding	moving in a restless fashion	30	totter grass	quaking grass	103
gads	gad fly	87	tutling	whistling, tootle	137
green ruffs	variety of gooseberry	113	wimble	gimlet, auger	43
harrif	stalks of cleavers	49	younkers	youngster	113
hazzle tassels	catkins	51			
heath bells	hare bells	50			

172

BIBLIOGRAPHY.

If this book has inspired you to know more about John Clare then I recommend the following for further reading.

Carry Ackroyd: Natures Powers and Spells, Langford Press 2009.

Jonathan Bate : John Clare : A Biography, Picador, 2005
John Clare : Selected Poems, Faber & Faber 2003

Ronald Blythe   At Helpston, Meetings with John Clare, Black Dog Books 2011
Talking About John Clare, Trent Books 1999

Edmund Blunden   Sketches in the Life of John Clare, 1931

Tim Chilcott   The Shepherd's Calendar, Carcanet 2006

Simon Kövesi   John Clare, Flower Poems, M&C Services, 2001
John Clare, Love Poems, M&C Services, 1999

Eric Robinson & David Powell
John Clare by Himself, Carcanet 1996
John Clare : Major Works, Oxford World's Classics 1984-2004

Eric Robinson & Geoffrey Summerfield
Clare, Selected Poems and Prose, Oxford University Press
1966.
Kelsey Thornton & Anne Tibble
The Midsummer Cushion, Midnag, Carcanet 1990

J.W. and Anne Tibble
John Clare a Life, Cobden~Sanderson Ltd 1932
John Clare, The Prose of, Routledge & Kegan Paul Ltd 1951
The Letters of John Clare, Routledge & Kegan Paul Ltd 1951

The John Clare Society publishes a quarterly newsletter and yearly Journal for their membership. They also have an excellent website :
http://www.johnclaresociety.blogspot.com.

A few Contact Details for Societies Protecting our
Wild Life and their Habitats.

...... There once were springs, where daisies' silver studs
Like sheets of snow on every pasture spread;
There once were summers, when the crow=flower buds
Like golden sunbeams brightest lustre shed;
And trees grew once that shelter'd Lubin's head;
There once were brooks sweet whimpering down the vale:
The brook's no more - kingcup and daisy fled;
Their last fall'n tree the naked moors bewail,
And scarce a bush is left to tell the mournful tale.

From 'The Village Minstrel' 1821

We are fortunate in this country to have dedicated people helping
to preserve and encourage participation in the conservation and
protection of our wildlife. They all rely on support both financially
and from volunteers to help with their work. Here are a few contact
details for the larger societies. The websites will have links to many
smaller groups of enthusiasts around the country with their own
specialities, and who will welcome your interest.

Campaign to Protect Rural England.   www-cpre.org.uk
National Office,
5-11, Lavington Street,
London SE1 ONZ

Countryside Restoration Trust,   www.countrysiderestorationtrust.com
Haslingfield Road,
Barton, Cambs. CB 23 7AQ

National Trust - www.nationaltrust.org.uk
P.O. Box 574,
Manvers,
Rotherham. S63 3FH

National Wildflower Centre - www.nwc.org.uk
Court Hey Park
Roby Road
Knowsley
Liverpool. L 16 3NA.

cont.

Natural England,   www.naturalengland.org.uk
Foundry House,
3, Millsands,
Riverside Exchange,
Sheffield   S3 8NH.

Royal Society for the Protection of Birds (RSPB) www.rspb.org.uk
The Lodge,
Potton Road,
Sandy,
Bedfordshire,   SG19 2DL

Woodland Trust — www.woodlandtrust.org.uk
Kempton Way,
Grantham,
Lincolnshire   NG31 6LL

*The Wildlife Trusts have 47 Wildlife Trusts covering the whole of the
UK and manage many hundreds of nature reserves. For details
of your nearest Trust, visit : www.wildlifetrusts.org
Wildlife Trusts,
The Kiln,
Mather Road,
Newark, Nottinghamshire. NG24 1WT.

* N. Charles Rothschild 1877-1923 was the inspirational founder and first
Chairman of The Society for the Promotion of Nature Reserves, that became
The Wildlife Trusts. He was also first cousin to Lionel, the creator of the
Gardens at Exbury, where the wild flowers for this book were painted.
George C. Druce who wrote The Flora of Northamptonshire researched
and wrote his book while staying at Charles' home at Ashton. The contents
for 'My Wild Field Catalogue of Flowers' p164-171 are from his book pub.1930.

   ...... Hardy clowns! grudge not the wheat
    Which hunger forces birds to eat :
    your blinded eyes, worst foes to you,
    can't see the good which sparrows do.
    Did not poor birds with watching rounds
    Pick up the insects from your grounds,
    Did they not tend the rising grain,
    You then might sow to reap in vain......
     From 'The Summer Evening'
      Poems Descriptive of Rural Life and
       Scenery 1820

~ COVER CONTENTS ~
~ Bird eggs ~

1. Robin *Erithacus rubecula*   2. Crested Tit *Parus cristatus*
3. Long-tailed Tit *Aegithalos caudatus*   4. Blackbird *Turdus merula*
5. Jackdaw *Corvus monedula*   6. Swallow *Hirundo rustica*
7. Yellowhammer *Emberiza citrinella*   8. Great Tit *Parus major*
9. Dunnock *Prunella modularis*   10. Nightingale *Luscinia megarhynchos*
11. Goldfinch *Carduelis carduelis*   12. Mistle Thrush, *Turdus viscivorus*
11a Blue tit *Parus caeruleus*
~ FLOWERS ~

13. Fritillary *Fritillaria meleagris*   14. Harebell *Campanula rotundifolia*
15. Wood Anemone *Anemone nemorosa*   16. Cuckoo Flower *Cardamine pratensis*
17. Sweet Violet *Viola odorata*   17a Common Dog Violet *Viola riviniana*
~ Butterflies ~

18. orange tip *Anthocharis cardamines* 19. Wood white *Leptidea sinapis*
20. Small skipper *Thymelicus sylvestris* 21. Buff-tailed bumble-bee *Bombus terrestris*

It is illegal to take eggs or disturb nesting birds. All egg paintings in this book are after F.W. Frohawk. c.1898.

ABANDONED NEST

So fragile in construction,
So delicate in nature,
So full of potential,
So vulnerable in its environment
So easily destroyed.

~ Orange-tip butterfly ~

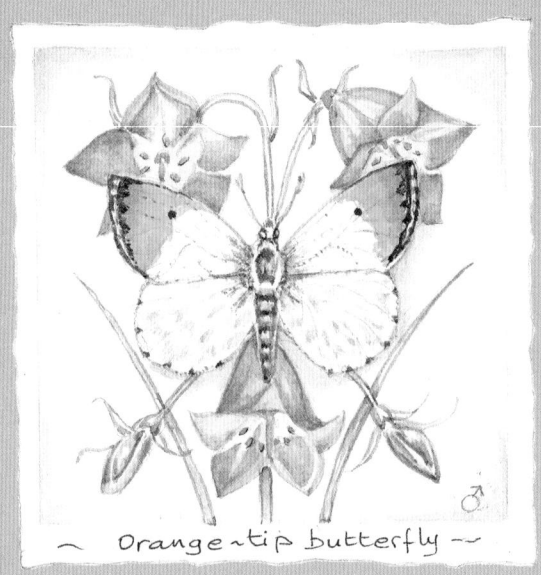

~ Orange~tip butterfly ~